Ordering Information:
You can purchase digital or print copies of this book at http://mpd.me

Printed in the United States of America
First Edition

Design by Andrea Goodlin

Author's Note

SINCE BECOMING A VENTURE CAPITALIST, I have been in awe of the many talented visionaries who have come in to pitch world-changing ideas. Many of these entrepreneurs are world-class business athletes and jacks of nearly every business trade. They're competent in product development, sales, marketing, finance, strategy and management, making them uniquely capable of weaving concepts and resources into a sustainable business.

What is shocking to me, however, is that many of the world's best entrepreneurs are bad at fundraising. At first, I didn't understand why, since the skills used in fundraising are many of the same skills used to create businesses. Over time, however, the reason these athletes underperform became clear. They don't possess a fundamental understanding of the fundraising process. They have the skills, but not the knowledge.

To take a step back, I would argue that it's not the fault of these entrepreneurs. Although they can easily evaluate the markets in which they want to launch their ventures, accessing the internal workings of these enigmatic investment institutions is not as easy. The only way to understand the inner workings of a venture fund is to become a venture capitalist, or to experience the fundraising process first-hand, multiple times, leaving even the best entrepreneurs to flail through their first few rounds.

My mission in writing this book is to illuminate the fundraising process so that engaging these venture capitalists is no longer like walking in the dark.

I will provide a detailed account of both the key steps in fundraising and the rationale behind them. The information should help entrepreneurs see through the eyes of the venture capital investor, enabling them to better understand motivations of investors and how best to engage them.

While this book does not cover every nuance of the process – entrepreneurs who read this will surely still tread over unexpected ground – this book should help them understand the lay of the land, significantly reducing the number of surprises.

While I believe that this book will be useful for entrepreneurs engaging in raising their second or third round of capital, it is primarily designed to assist entrepreneurs seeking their Seed or Series A investment, as they should accumulate a board of experienced investors thereafter which can help them negotiate future capital raises.

I do not view this book as a betrayal of the arcane art of venture investing. Rather, I hope that this tool will make the life of a venture investor easier. Entrepreneurs who understand the fundraising process are more likely to be prepared to answer questions investors will have, provide the materials that investors require and facilitate the process more effectively. In sum, it is my hope that this guide will simplify the role of the investors, taking some of the friction out of the process.

My intended audience for this book is the entrepreneur. There are, however, other groups that may find this helpful. Aspiring VCs may use this document to understand many of the nuances of the venture investment process, while agents for startup companies may also be more prepared to serve their clients having digested the knowledge herein.

Lastly, this book is written for all skill levels. I attempted to cover most of the topics that an entrepreneur should understand, regardless of how basic the topic may be, to ensure that new entrepreneurs are able to find the foundational information required to prepare for this process. As a result, more experienced entrepreneurs may find that some sections of this book cover topics they already understand. For this reason, I arranged the topics covered into discrete sections, enabling experienced entrepreneurs to quickly navigate to sections of interest, avoiding the more mundane. Furthermore, this structure ensures that this reference guide can quickly be leveraged to find key information as it becomes relevant to entrepreneurs throughout their fundraising endeavors.

Lastly, to the entrepreneur reading this: Go get 'em.

Acknowledgements

I am indebted to my closest VC mentors, the inspirational Jed Katz and the wise Thatcher Bell, for their guidance and support throughout this endeavor. They provided me with numerous topics, context and spellchecking — without which, this would not have been possible (or coherent).

This book also owes its existence to the managerial skills of Samman, the editorial detail of Danielle Fankhauser and the overly talented artistic eye of Andrea Goodlin.

A special thank you goes to my business partners for tolerating this pet project. Last but not least, to my wife, Laurie. Without her constant forgiveness this book would never have been completed.

Disclaimer

ONCE UPON A TIME, I BUMPED INTO ANOTHER VC who was an avid reader of my blog. He mentioned that his firm's fundraising process varies in some ways from what I describe in my writing. I wasn't surprised by this, and I want to make sure readers of this book aren't surprised, either.

Each VC fund is different. Funds have distinct cultures, investment strategies and investment processes. The objective of this book is not to characterize the fundraising process at every VC fund. Not only would that be impossible, it would make for a boring read.

Instead, I am trying to describe what I believe is a relatively generic process. I will do my best to highlight areas where I see significant variation. As a result, you should understand that this book provides general guidance and therefore, seek to discover the nuances of the process for each fund.

new investment at a new valuation. While, in theory, the value of a successful portfolio company is constantly increasing, the value was only changed on the books periodically – at the time of a valuation event. Since portfolio companies typically raise additional capital 12 - 24 months after their first investment, their valuations were not updated frequently. More recently, accounting rules for private companies have changed to encourage VCs to adjust valuations more frequently, commensurate with significant developments for portfolio companies. Even so, accountants and VCs tend to be conservative in their valuations of successful portfolio companies.

Second, companies that don't succeed often shut down relatively quickly. They burn through their cash and are unable to raise more money since they haven't demonstrated enough progress.

As a result, less successful companies are written down or off quickly before the successful companies are written up, creating a distortion that appears to be a loss of money.

VENTURE FUND ECONOMICS: A FEW COMPANIES GENERATE THE PORTFOLIO'S RETURN

Every time VCs make an investment, they believe the company they are backing will generate a healthy return. In reality, that's not the case.

Even the most successful early-stage investors experience failure rates in their portfolios, which are probably surprising to people not familiar with the business. A rule of thumb for top-performing investors is that one third of their investments will "go to zero," one third will return the invested capital and one third will provide a five to tenfold return. Furthermore, in the early-stage model, the few companies that return 10 times or more on invested capital provide the vast majority of the fund's total return to its investors (who are called limited partners).

This reality has implications for entrepreneurs who are raising an early round of venture capital. First, you need to convince investors that your company can generate a big return, since VCs need to make every investment with the belief that it will do so. Second, you should expect the market valuation for your company to be lower than initial intuition tells you. Since two-thirds of the companies which receive venture investments generate mediocre returns for early stage investors, investors likely perceive the riskiness of your venture to be higher than you will.

VC FINANCIAL PERFORMANCE REQUIREMENTS

I have been asked what revenue and EBITDA are required to receive investment. The answer to this question (as with many others) is, it depends.

First, the sector likely serves as a significant determinant of the necessary revenue and profit. It typically takes less capital to get an IT company to market than a pharmaceutical company. As a result, it's likely that financial performance expectations at each round of investment vary. While Series B investments in pharmaceutical companies may be done with no expectation of revenue, most (but not all) healthy IT companies seeking a Series B investment have revenue.

Second, within a sector, investment strategies of VC funds vary substantially. There are several funds in the tri-state area that target Series A investments in companies with at least $5 million of revenue. Others will do Series A rounds with companies that do not have revenue.

When thinking about the financial requirements of each type of fund, it's worthwhile to think about the other implied aspects of their investment strategy. A fund's financial requirements are an indicator of risk tolerance. Funds that invest in pre-revenue companies are generally willing to take bigger risks. Also (because risk tolerances vary), return requirements also vary. Firms that take more risk by investing pre-revenue generally seek higher returns.

To give a sense of the relationship between risk and return profiles: VCs who invest in pre-revenue or early revenue companies commonly target 10x plus returns, while VCs investing in companies with at least $5 million of revenue often seek 3x to 6x returns.

You might note that IRR requirements are not so widely variant, but the longer the holding period, the larger the multiple to achieve the same IRR. Revenue/profit are predictors of holding period.

In sum, investment strategies vary substantially by fund. Be sure you target VCs who have an investment thesis that is aligned with your company.

DON'T PLAN ON BUYING VCS OUT

I have heard entrepreneurs ask if it's typical for management to buy VCs out of the capitalization table after the company has free cash flow. These entrepreneurs are thinking they could give the VC their original investment plus a fair market return in exchange for their equity.

First and foremost, you need to understand that if you take capital from a VC you will typically not have the right to buy out the VCs. While situations in which the company buys the equity from one or more parties (a stock buyback or recapitalization), or where two private parties engage in a transaction (a secondary transaction) do take place, the company (or management) cannot force an investor to shed their holding in a company.

Furthermore, it's worth noting that VCs typically do not liquidate their investment via stock buybacks or secondary transactions – these arrangements are the exception, not the rule. Most VCs seek to liquidate their investment through a merger or IPO. There's good reason for this – M&A and IPO transactions usually generate better returns than buyback or secondary transactions. A sale to another company captures a control premium and IPO makes the equity accessible to many more buyers, often driving up the price.

The main takeaway here is that if you pursue venture capital, assume that your investors will be involved with your company until the company goes under or until you have an exit.

Behind the Scenes

THE MARKET FOR VENTURE CAPITAL

On occasion, I hear people imply that VCs take too big of a cut in a venture transaction. While this cut can come in the form of participation and liquidity preference, at the end of the day, some perceive the share of potential returns apportioned to VCs are too big – implying unfairness is inherent to the transaction.

I understand that different people will place different values on the contributions of a venture capitalist (capital and beyond), but it's important to understand that the VC's cut is allocated by market dynamics – a two-sided market.

1. **Market for investable capital:** This is the market between venture capitalists and the institutions that provide them capital.
2. **Market for investments:** This is the market between venture capital investors and startups.

As I will discuss, these markets are interrelated.

THE MARKET FOR VENTURE CAPITAL: INVESTABLE CAPITAL

The first side of that market is the market for investable capital, referring to the market for capital that VCs need to raise in order to invest it in startups. As described above, venture capitalists typically get their funding from institutions, such as pension funds and universities. Like VCs, these institutions create portfolios of investments, of which venture capital is often only one category or asset class.

These portfolios are divided into pools of capital, allocated to traditional assets (e.g., public stocks and bonds) and alternative assets (e.g., hedge funds, leveraged buyout and venture capital). While some institutions earmark portions of their portfolio for venture capital, many only decide what portion will be allocated to alternative assets, leaving the various types of alternative asset managers (e.g., hedge funds, leveraged buyout and venture capital) to duke it out for a share of the pie.

While institutions evaluate alternative asset managers based on a number of criteria, it is not surprising that returns play a key role in determining whether or not a manager gets the investment. As a result, when VCs make investments in their portfolio companies, they are investing with an eye toward realizing the type of overall portfolio return that they need in order to generate the competitive return that will enable them to raise their next funds.

In sum, the performance of other alternative asset classes and the return expectations of institutions drive VC return objectives.

THE MARKET FOR VENTURE CAPITAL: INVESTMENTS

The second side of the market for venture capital is the market for investments, where VCs jockey to get money into startups and vice versa.

One force in this market is simple supply and demand. If there are lots of VCs bidding for a startup, the terms of the eventual investment are likely to be more favorable to the entrepreneur. Similarly, if there is only one VC interested the terms are more likely to be favorable to the VC.

Additionally, substitution plays an important role in this market. If there are lots of great startups chasing a limited number of financiers, a VC may be able to get a better deal.

Another way of looking at the market is the risk-return ratio. Investing in startups is an inherently risky business, even for investors with a good eye. There are lots of exogenous risks that might undercut a perfectly reasonable venture along the way. Nothing shocking here – VCs need to own enough of the company to ensure that they are compensated for the risk they are taking – higher returns are required to offset the high risk of losing everything.

THE MARKET FOR VENTURE CAPITAL: THE RELATIONSHIP BETWEEN THE TWO MARKETS

Each market has independent forces driving valuations, but they are interrelated. When you think about the dynamics driving fluctuations in the market for investments, it's important to realize the role of the market for investable capital. VCs need to generate returns competitive with other alternative asset classes (e.g., hedge funds and leveraged buyout shops). In order to generate sufficient returns, they have a minimum threshold on the valuation that they can accept in their investments.

This minimum brings a few implications.

- First, favorable negotiating dynamics can impact valuation, but only by so much.
- Second, the comment that VCs generally take too big a cut in a transaction reflects a lack of understanding of the underlying cost of capital – VC is just the next best option an institutional investor has in the alternative asset class.

VCS ARE SET UP TO BE BAD GUYS

There is a lot of animosity towards VCs, even the good ones.

The industry is designed in a way that forces them to be portrayed as bad guys more often than not. In order to do their jobs well, most VCs are forced to fund less than one percent of the companies they see. They're saying "no" to most of the entrepreneurs they meet (no matter how much they like the people). To make matters worse, entrepreneurs have an emotional attachment to their business ideas – they consider their companies to be their babies. As a result, they often take criticism personally.

If you put these two facts together, a successful VC must offend (to some degree) 99 percent of the entrepreneurs they meet. Imagine if you lived in a world where you had to tell 99 percent of the moms that you meet that their babies are ugly. It's an unfortunate part of the job, to say the least.

The takeaway for entrepreneurs is that they shouldn't take rejection too personally. The venture process can be painful because there are numerous factors that influence a VCs decision – even good startups receive a fair amount of rejection. Nobody likes this part of the process – not even the VCs.

THE VENTURE POLICE: REPUTATION

Some entrepreneurs seem to wonder what keeps VCs honest. From their perspective, VCs don't have anyone keeping them in check. This couldn't be further from the truth. Everyone is keeping them honest.

VC is a relationship business. If limited partners (those who invest in VC funds) or entrepreneurs think a VC is a scoundrel, that person won't see new deals and won't be able to raise another fund – their days as a VC will be numbered. This is a very real and powerful pressure that impacts VCs. While not every VC takes these pressures seriously enough, the good ones get it.

As a result, the best VCs do right by entrepreneurs and others. What this means is, they are pretty good about keeping their word and being honest.

The Exit

There are four types of exits that a VC will pursue during the course of an investment: mergers and acquisitions, IPO, secondary, and recapitalization.

MERGERS & ACQUISITIONS (#1)

In an acquisition, one company buys another, taking a controlling stake of its shares and rights to assets. While these deals are structured in a number of ways and selecting a structure involves numerous considerations, the key variables boil down to: 1) whether or not the buyer takes on the liabilities of the company being acquired, and 2) the types of assets being used to purchase the company (e.g., cash or stock).

In a merger, two companies are combined, each being treated an equal, more or less. While combinations called mergers happen all the time, it is rare that they are actually mergers of equals. Even if the financial structure portrays a picture of two equal companies being combined, one of the two parties typically takes control of the other, in one way or another. Most often, control is determined by the board or management structure. The CEO who is selected to lead the combined entity keeps all of his or her lieutenants around, squeezing out the other company's management team.

Most VC exits (especially in recent years) are realized when portfolio companies are acquired by larger, often public, cash-rich companies. These transactions are structured such that the buyer assumes the portfolio company's liabilities. Venture investors expect this, as they do not want to be responsible for paying off debt after the transaction.

Additionally, VCs have a strong preference for selling portfolio companies for cash, rather than shares of the acquiring company. There is good reason for this preference: the value of the buyer's shares can change over time, reducing the effective purchase price. Furthermore, if a buyer elects to pay with its shares, its management may believe that their company's shares are overvalued.

M&A: EARN-OUTS: DISTRIBUTING RISK

When acquirers and the shareholders of a company come to an impasse on valuation based on assumptions about future performance, the pricing gap is sometimes bridged through an earn-out. An earn-out is when the buyer agrees to pay current shareholders additional compensation as pre-determined operating metrics are achieved in the future.

For example, if shareholders expect sales to increase next year and the acquirer doesn't, the acquirer might agree to pay more for the company in the future if sales do, in fact, increase. Doing so enables the acquirer to protect itself from paying too much for the target, and in the event that sales don't increase, the seller takes on the performance risk.

While structures vary greatly, in the plain vanilla version, the target is purchased for a base price with the possibility of an additional earn-out. Earn-outs need to be well defined to ensure that both parties know when the payouts are triggered.

Sellers try to avoid earn-outs because it requires them to assume the performance risk. However, earn-outs are not uncommon as they are a useful mechanism for allocating risk.

M&A: THE CONTROL PREMIUM

When a portfolio company is acquired, the buyer is expected to pay more per share than a minority investor would. There is good reason for this – the buyer is getting more than the investor. The buyer is purchasing the right to control the company. After an acquisition, a buyer can determine a company's strategy, select which markets to focus on, select the company's partners, elect which assets to sell, change the company's level of debt, and so on. An investor can influence these decisions, but not control them outright.

Acquisition prices are generally higher than prices for investment rounds, reflecting a control premium.

IPO (#2)

IPO, or initial public offering, is another of the four types of exits. In an initial public offering, a company first sells a portion of it shares in a public market, such as the NY Stock Exchange or the NASDAQ.

By going public, a company sells a portion of its stock to investors who are entitled to freely sell their shares over the specified exchange. Through the exchange, they can sell directly or indirectly to virtually any buyer in the world.

It's worth noting that not all of the company's stock is publicly accessible at the IPO. Companies typically sell only a portion of the company to investors through the public exchanges.

What makes IPOs so special is that subsequent public offerings are less risky for the company. Once shares are being freely traded and priced by the market, the company has more information about the stock's pricing. During the IPO, the company's investment bankers are tasked with creating a small marketplace and identifying clearing prices for the initial shares. After those shares are sold, the buyers can transact them freely, yielding prices that reflect the valuation applied by more buyers and sellers, creating a price that is truly reflective of the market's estimate of the company's value.

VCs, entrepreneurs and others often participate in the public offering, meaning that they include their shares in the group that is sold to the market. This enables VCs to exit at least a part of their investment – shares are converted into cash, which can be distributed to their limited partners.

VCs generally like exiting through IPOs. While IPOs present investors with some liquidity risk, as insiders are often subjected to lock-up periods (during which the investors and entrepreneurs cannot sell their shares on the market, immediately after the IPO), IPOs offer VCs several advantages. First, public companies remain going concerns, enabling VCs to take credit for investments that they made (potentially) long into the future. An IPO not only offers a VC a merit badge that can be promoted to entrepreneurs and limited partners, but it also enables the VC to leverage its contacts at the newly public company to help future portfolio companies in many ways (from acquiring customers and partners to initiating acquisitions).

IPOS USUALLY TAKE LONGER TO REALIZE THAN M&A

The average company exiting through a public offering is more mature than a company that exits through an acquisition, at least since 2000.

There is good reason for this extra maturation. Public investors are often seeking to buy shares in companies that will continue to operate independently long into the future. In contrast, corporate acquirers may buy companies when they are very young, before the company has demonstrated the ability to sustain itself. There are a variety of reasons that a company is bought without demonstrating financial sustainability; a fledgling company might be acquired for its assets (technology, customer, contracts or management) or it may be acquired as a defensive maneuver to eliminate the opportunity for the company to become a long-term threat.

It could also be argued that Sarbanes-Oxley legislation, which requires additional internal process documentation and oversight by public companies traded on U.S. exchanges, has delayed public offerings. Companies must ensure that they will be compliant with Sarbanes-Oxley regulations, and that they are able to afford associated costs before they can issue public stock for the first time.

From 1996 to 2008, the average company that IPO'd was eight months older than the average company to be acquired. It's worth noting that this pattern didn't hold true during the Internet boom. In the period of 1996 to 1999, the average software company making its initial public offering was five months younger than the average company being acquired (according to data from Dow Jones Venture One).

This general trend of IPOs taking longer to realize than acquisition also puts pressure on investors to push for larger exit values. VCs are judged by their investors based on several metrics, one of which is called the Internal Rate of Return (IRR). An IRR is an accurate way of measuring the average annual rate of return on invested capital adjusted for the timing of cash flows. A simple relationship that comes from this math is the fact that longer times to exit reduce the effective annual return. Returning 200 percent of invested dollars in one year implies a higher average annual increase in value than returning 200 percent of invested dollars in 10 years. As a result, the delay in exit time drives VCs to require higher exit values to adjust for the delay. While, in theory, the increase in value can be justified by the company's ability to expand its operations and increase revenues over that period, every exit is ultimately a negotiation and this delay drives VCs to target higher exit values.

IMPACT OF THE LONGER TIME TO EXIT FOR BOTH M&A AND IPO

An important trend is taking place in the venture marketplace – it is taking longer for VCs to exit their investments.

In 1995 (before the Internet boom), the average software acquisition occurred 48 months after a company was launched. Initial public offerings were made at an average of 56 months into a venture. In 2007, M&A happened on month no. 65 and IPOs on month no. 67. That's a significant change – 35 percent and 20 percent later, respectively.

Will this trend reverse over time? If the time to exit continues to lengthen, we could see a number of consequences. Some of the potential impacts include:

- **Longer LP commitments:** Venture funds are designed in such a way that limited partners are required to commit capital for about 10 years. However, with an average five and a half years to IPO, there are bound to be companies that don't exit for up to a decade, meaning that LPs may be required to commit their capital for a longer period.

- **Increased liquidity premium:** LPs agree to lock up capital in a venture fund for up to 10 years due to the expectation that the risk taken in having the capital tied up (which may mean they miss future investment opportunities) is compensated for by higher returns. If the lock-up period increases, LPs will likely demand a higher return (or they'll invest their money elsewhere such as hedge funds or leverage buyout firms).

- **Lower valuations:** If VCs across the board need to generate higher returns (and they can't increase their time to exit) they will require greater ownership of their portfolio companies, translating into lower valuations of startups and greater dilution of entrepreneurs.

This scenario is a losing situation for everyone and I am optimistic that the market will evolve back to shorter exit times as the M&A and IPO markets enter future legs of their cycles. However, it's important to continue to watch these dynamics, as they could have industry-wide consequences.

SECONDARY (#3)

In a secondary transaction, shares are sold by individual shareholders to a third-party buyer. Note that this differs from an investment since the shares are not being sold by the company. In essence, this is structured like a side deal whereby one shareholder is able to realize liquidity without changing the number of shares or cash position.

Secondary transactions happen for one of two reasons. First, employees who worked at a startup for a number of years may want to liquidate a portion of their shares to get some cash out of the venture, before the company is acquired or has an IPO. Secondaries are also frequently leveraged by investors who are either in need of cash to meet other commitments or who need to liquidate their assets because they are at the end of their fund's life cycle.

Secondary transactions are generally considered less attractive than an acquisition or IPO. One reason is simply the fact that these do not represent a company-wide exit, meaning this type of exit presents a less sexy story in the track record of founders and investors – the fate of the company may not yet be determined at the time of the transaction. Another reason for this comes from the fact that buyers in a secondary transaction generally understand that

FRIENDS AND FAMILY

F&F capital is the starting point of a company, often used for basic administrative details including corporate formation, market research and the creation of a business plan.

- Typical round size: Can be as small as $5,000 and as large as $500,000
- Investment structure: Convertible note or common stock
- Hurdle for next stage: Business plan and management team

Seed

Seed investments are provided to companies that have a business plan and a management team, but do not yet have a product. At this point, companies are raising money based upon an idea and a team.
- Typical round size: $500,000 – $2 million
- Investment structure: Convertible note or common stock
- Hurdle for next stage: Product

Series A

The word "Series" implies institutional money (money invested by a VC). The letter "A" means that it is the first institutional round. Note that Seed rounds, especially in the IT sector, are increasingly being led by institutional investors, which makes the name "Series A" a bit of a misnomer. By the Series A, most companies have a product that is ready (or close to ready) to take to market.

- Typical round size: These are typically $2 - $5 million (but can be as little as $1 million and as large as $10 million).
- Investment structure: Participating preferred stock
- Hurdle for next stage: Market adoption

Series B

In order to raise a Series B, the company needs to have demonstrated market traction, be further developed the business and have recruited a more robust management team.

- Typical round size: These are typically $5 - $10 million but (can be as little as $5 million and as large as $25 million).
- Investment structure: Participating preferred stock
- Hurdle for next stage: Growth

Series C and Beyond

After the Series B round, the required achievements vary by company. Some companies are nowhere near profitability and need more capital to stay alive, and others are profitable but need capital in order to accelerate growth.

THE FUNDRAISING CADENCE FOR TECH-LIGHT COMPANIES

Exceptions to every rule exist, but there are some strong guidelines when it comes to
development milestones for tech-light IT startups at each stage of venture capital funding.

Before I continue, a few clarifications:

1. These guidelines don't necessarily apply to other sectors or heavy technology startups.
2. This process only applies to companies that pursue venture financing.

These milestones are the overarching objectives that an entrepreneur should pursue to get to the next round of financing. Although meeting or failing to meet these milestones does not determine whether or not a company will receive their next round of funding (as both idiosyncratic and systemic risks can impact the financing outcome), these proof points generally provide investors with the key pieces of information that inform the investment decision at each stage. As a result, hitting these milestones increases the odds that you'll be able to secure your next tranche of capital.

The required milestones to raise a given type of financing are as follows:

Friends & Family
- A draft business plan
- One or more founders

Seed
- A more refined business plan, including early indications of the marketing equation (cost of customer acquisition and customer lifetime value) and a financial model
- A more complete founding team
- A prototype technology

Series A

- A developed business plan that reflects a relatively detailed understanding of how to scale the company (often with some proof points in how to scale the company)
- A team that has its key team members
- A scalable working technology
- Early customer traction and revenue

Series B

- A demonstrable method for scaling the business going forward
- A deeper management team that has increased specialization across roles
- An increasingly robust technology
- A rapidly-growing revenue run rate

Beyond the Series B the typical use case of capital is for growing the business by continuing to pour fuel into an increasingly refined engine.

Again, while all companies vary in their development, these overarching milestones can help entrepreneurs understand the proof points that they should seek to achieve in order to de-risk their startups sufficiently for their next financing.

SEED MILESTONE: BUILD THE ENGINE

By the time most entrepreneurs take in seed money, they're champing at the bit to expand their customer base as quickly as possible. While that intuitively seems like the right thing, in some situations, it may not be.

For companies looking for venture scale, entrepreneurs should focus on proving out key milestones between each financing. This enables them to stay in the fundraising cadence – likely taking friction out of the capital raising process. While I'm a believer that rules are meant to be broken and all things come in shades of gray, the general milestones for entrepreneurs to hit between financings are guidelines worth following.

For founders of information companies who are taking a seed investment in preparation for a Series A financing, ramping their customer base as fast as possible may not be the right move. One of the most important milestones to hit before the Series A financing is quantification of marketing metrics in scalable marketing channels. In English, that means understanding how much it costs to acquire customers in a scalable fashion. Here's the takeaway – there can be a big difference between understanding how you can scale your user base and actually scaling it.

For many entrepreneurs, there are ways to acquire new customers with a bit of hustle that can't be done at scale. Going to conferences, emailing friends and knocking on doors may be great ways to get early adopters, but often aren't scalable activities. While these aren't bad methods, it's pretty common for entrepreneurs to spend all or most of their seed money doing just these activities upfront, since they know these often are the easiest acquisition channels.

Here's the problem – if you go this route, when you go to raise your Series A, you probably won't be able to look investors in the eye and tell them the right channels and associated acquisition costs for scaling your user base 10 or 100 times. While you might be able to show customer adoption, you might not actually know how to grow.

Here's a metaphor for how I think about this. Imagine starting a company is like a race. A seed round will only give a startup so much time to make progress. I think entrepreneurs can use that time in one of two ways. First, they can choose to put on their running shoes and start covering ground or they can stay back in the shop a little while longer building an engine for a race car. As an investor, I would rather make a Series A investment in a company that understands how all of the gears fit together and has an engine ready to ramp than a company that sprinted its first lap and is getting tired.

As a result, I think it's important for entrepreneurs to focus on testing scalable marketing channels early and aggressively, even if it means flatter adoption curves and higher initial acquisition costs. The key is to build the engine so you can pour in Series A fuel and press on the gas.

THE FUNDRAISING PROCESS IS FLEXIBLE

As aforementioned, there are generic milestones for each stage in the fundraising process. While these milestones should provide some guidance, the process can vary greatly for each company.

Be flexible. When designing your fundraising strategy, simply try to do what would be best for building your company. However, you may find that investors don't agree with your approach. As a result, you need to be prepared to be flexible and change course if all of the investors recommend (or require) a different process, meaning that more milestones are hit before a specific financing round can be completed.

a very poor return – lots of money is spent to yield very little additional profit. And, what's worse is that the capital that was re-invested could have been paid to the founders.

Furthermore, when the company is sold at a low value (since the company did not have the DNA to scale to a meaningful size) the liquidity preference will consume a significant percentage of the exit value, potentially leaving very little for the founders. This scenario is further exacerbated as the original strategy fails to scale, because additional capital will need to be raised in order to explore new business strategies to increase the outstanding liquidity preference and further reducing the payout for the founders.

It's worth noting that the venture capital model works very well for companies poised to scale, but is disastrous when applied to companies with less potential. As a result, it is critical that founders seek to understand the potential of their business and capitalize it properly. If you have a company that will not scale, do not raise venture capital.

COMMON FINANCING MISTAKES: BOOTSTRAPPING YOUR COMPANY TO DEATH

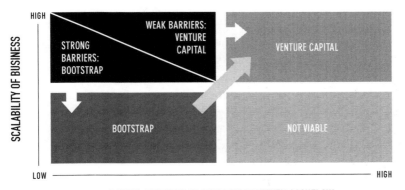

We have all heard the glamorous stories of entrepreneurs becoming billion-aires by maxing out their credit cards and launching startups out of their garages. It does happen, but for every success story there are many more failures. While this doesn't mean that entrepreneurs should cower from a challenge, there are lessons to be learned about how to mitigate some of the risk in the venture.

Entrepreneurs should not over-extend their personal finances when starting a company.

While this advice does run counter to the financing strategies prevalent in entrepreneur folklore, I agree with it. When an entrepreneur assumes too much personal financial distress, he loses the ability to invest time in building a business. Put another way, as a person approaches bankruptcy, they lose freedom to be entrepreneurial. If a mountain of credit card payments are looming, you may need to get a day job, slowing the development of your company.

As a result, it's important for entrepreneurs to be thoughtful about avoiding personal financial distress early in the development of their company. If you have the assets to self-fund the company with ease, you won't have a problem. If you don't, you may want to seek third party capital early on.

WANT VC? BE READY TO GO BIG

The size of exit should also dictate whether an entrepreneur takes the VC route. Generally speaking, venture capitalists need their portfolio companies to exit for very large values in order to meaningfully impact their returns. Typically this means eight- or, better yet, nine-figure exits (tens or hundreds of millions of dollars) are required to "move the needle."

As a result, VCs may often opt to pass up opportunities to sell their portfolio companies that are showing strong potential for seven or even eight-figure valuations – they'll want to hold out for the bigger exit. Doing so usually helps maximize returns for all parties (including the entrepreneur); however, it requires more patience and a stronger stomach for risk.

Further to this point, VCs structure their investments using liquidity preference to align incentives – compelling the entrepreneur to hold out for the big win. Taking all this into account, entrepreneurs should know that getting into bed with a VC typically means setting your sights on going big – very big. If you're looking for a small lifestyle business or a small exit, venture capital is probably not right for you.

OTHER REASONS TO RAISE MONEY FROM VCS

If you're starting a venture scale business, raising money from venture capitalists early in the life of the company can be a great idea. While securing capital is important, however, the money isn't the only reason to engage in the VC fundraising process. There are a number of other benefits.

- **Enhance the plan:** By pitching to VCs and getting feedback, an entrepreneur receives valuable feedback that helps to refine the business model, marketing strategy and other aspects of his plan.

- **Make connections:** While VCs don't make introductions for every entrepreneur they meet, entrepreneurs will likely be connected to important customers, partners and future members of their teams through the investment community.

- **Learn how to pitch the company:** By pitching early in the life of the company and pitching often, entrepreneurs learn how to sell their companies. From this perspective, selling in this way is not only important in fundraising, but is also critical for making key hires, securing partnerships and literally selling the company when the right buyer comes knocking.

FRINGE COMPANIES: BOOTSTRAP OR VENTURE CAPITAL?

Figuring out how to finance a company is easier for some founders than others. The choice is difficult when a business could make a great lifestyle business or a great venture-scale business. To clarify, this is a somewhat unique situation, as many startups are either not viable as small lifestyle businesses or do not have the potential to achieve venture scale. I call companies that could become either of these fringe companies.

To clarify, by lifestyle business I'm referring to smaller businesses (typically less than $10 million in annual sales at peak) that the founders don't intend to sell; rather, they intend to extract profits from the business in perpetuity. A venture-scale business is one that grows to much more than $10 million in annual revenue and has real potential to ramp to $100 million or more.

When faced with this dilemma, many entrepreneurs assume that they can simply raise venture capital in order to chase the bigger opportunity initially and fall back to the lifestyle business strategy if the company doesn't scale. More money appears to create the most real options – the founder gets to chase the upside case and still benefit from the downside case if things don't go as planned.

Here's the catch – taking venture capital in this scenario has two key implications:

1. It is likely you will not be able to operate the company as a lifestyle business if it doesn't scale (you'll likely be required to sell the company), and
2. Your return when selling the company in the downside scenario may be smaller than if you had bootstrapped it to the same size.

Here's why: Since venture capitalists must return invested capital to their investors, they need a method of exiting their investments. Typically, when a company stops growing, investors will work with the entrepreneurs to either seek more capital to explore new business opportunities that can stimulate growth (which usually means that the entrepreneur has a smaller portion of the pie) or find a buyer for the company. In either scenario, the company remains on the path to an exit, and entrepreneurs don't get the opportunity to run the company as a lifestyle business. Simply put, raising VC and chasing the upside case typically eliminates the option to have a lifestyle business.

Furthermore, by taking venture capital financing, the entrepreneur's ownership stake is diluted. The entrepreneur's share of any sale proceeds is therefore lower than if he had not taken venture financing. This is a fair trade for a venture-scale business, which probably achieves an optimal exit value only through the benefit of relatively large, fast infusions of capital that venture firms can provide. In this instance, the entrepreneur is getting a "smaller piece of a much larger pie." But for a lifestyle business, particularly one that might have become profitable without venture financing, the dilution entailed in venture financing is probably not a good trade for the entrepreneur.

While venture capital gives entrepreneurs the chance to make lots of money by building big companies, it's generally not designed to make founders wealthy for starting small companies. Bootstrapping a small company, however, can make founders quite wealthy.

Here's a simple diagram that illustrates the payout scenarios for fringe companies.

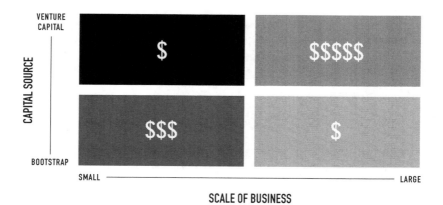

Founders with uncertain future market sizes are the most typical victims of this dilemma. In situations where the market is small today but expected to rapidly grow, the potential scale of a venture is more difficult to predict.

At the heart of this issue is an information gap – if you don't know how big a business can get, it is difficult to choose a financing strategy. You won't understand the potential scalability of the company until after you raise venture capital and commit to go big or go home.

One way to unravel this issue is to wait on the decision to raise venture capital until knowing the extent to which the company is scalable. For many entrepreneurs, the timing of capital needs won't afford this luxury, and for others, the prospect of delaying the capital raise is anxiety-provoking. If, however, you can test the market and better understand scalability before charting a financing strategy, this may maximize your return.

THE WRONG REASONS TO PURSUE VENTURE CAPITAL: SALARIES AND PERSONAL CREDIBILITY

There are a lot of good reasons for entrepreneurs pursue venture capital, including scaling your company more rapidly, developing complex technologies or entering new markets. There are, however, bad reasons to pursue venture capital.

Two of the most common wrong reasons to pursue venture capital are the pursuit of a steady paycheck for the founders and personal credibility.

Raising VC for the sole purpose of obtaining a salary is not the right approach. Raising venture capital is commitment to far more than just raising money; it's a commitment to manage your company for growth (not profits) and to work towards ends consistent with the needs of your venture partners. If all you need is a suitable salary, you may be able to achieve this objective by raising smaller amounts of capital from angels or non-traditional capital sources, which may require less of a shift in your business strategy. Or, better yet, build your business to provide sufficient profit to pay yourself what you deserve.

To be clear, as I stated above, I don't believe that founders should expose themselves to financial distress in pursuing their venture, as doing so can put their endeavor at risk. While founders should receive salaries, they should pursue capital sources that align with their needs. If the only need is some cash for founder salaries, other sources are almost certainly more suitable.

Although obtaining venture backing can give your company substantial credibility, this is also a faulty reason. On one hand, partners and customers may be more comfortable working with a venture-backed company due to the role VCs play in strengthening governance and providing financial stability. However, for some entrepreneurs, receiving venture backing is simply a form of validation – an indication that their efforts are not crazy, or they're not spending time in vain. Raising VC provides a big "I told you so" to skeptics. There is a difference, however, between seeking credibility for your company and for yourself. If you are more suited to succeed in your venture by raising angel money or other types of capital, don't pursue venture capital just for the personal validation that it provides.

Additional Capital Concerns

WHAT IS DUMB MONEY?

There are challenges associated with trying to raise a large sum of money from VCs in one round. In sum, if the capital raise is too large you will most likely give away too much ownership in your company, or scare off the VCs because they can't meet their ownership requirements. There's not enough of the company to go around.

There is another way. You could raise "dumb money."

I generally hate the name "dumb money" – it is a bit insulting, after all. As my mom would say, "It just isn't nice." There are, however, two reasons why it has that name. First, the phrase "dumb money" is first and foremost used to imply that the investors will not be able to add any value to the business beyond providing capital. They can't offer relevant advice or connections.

Second, dumb money is often invested in atypical structures that can both 1) reduce the odds of the investor generating a risk-adjusted return and 2) mitigate the entrepreneur's ability to raise subsequent capital. Put another way, dumb money can leave your company overvalued, scaring away future investors.

Don't be fooled: dumb money rarely comes from dumb people. More often than not, the investors who fall into this category are very successful businesspeople who simply made their money outside of the venture community (they aren't entrepreneurs, venture lawyers or early-stage investors). As a result, they're not as connected to the venture community and don't understand how to structure early-stage investments so that the entrepreneurs are poised to "stay in the system," meaning raise capital from investors who participate at various stages in the startup life cycle.

SHOULD YOU TAKE DUMB MONEY?

The fact that dumb money has a derogatory name implies that those who espouse conventional wisdom would urge you not to take it. While I believe few decisions in life are truly black and white, the answer to this question, "Should

At the end of the day, if you want to raise money you need to be prepared to share your business plan. If you're not ready to do that yet, keep your head down and develop your company to the point you are comfortable discussing it.

THE BENEFITS OF SHARING YOUR IDEA

While there is limited downside in sharing ideas with investors, there are often some significant benefits.

The most obvious benefit is the feedback that VCs can provide. By seeing many of the startups in the marketplace, VCs generally develop a wealth of knowledge that can be helpful to entrepreneurs. This can take many forms. Here are a few things VCs can do:

- Leverage best practices that they have seen to offer you advice about how to execute (e.g., sales, marketing, development strategies)
- Suggest partnerships or services that might enhance your business model, enabling you to take advantage of budding technologies
- Recommend other startups or mature companies with which you might partner in order to fill gaps in your operation or product offering
- Identify key challenges in your model based upon what they know about the nature of your market or based upon pitfalls that they have seen other companies encounter
- Introduce you to potential employees, partners, service providers and even other investors
- Provide feedback from an investor standpoint, enabling you to enhance your pitch
- Offer new ideas that may compliment your business model

The other benefit of sharing your idea with VCs, and sharing it early, comes from your ability to demonstrate a trend and engage in pre-marketing.

Your Target Structure

SHOULD YOU TRANCHE YOUR FUNDRAISING?

It's not uncommon for entrepreneurs to try to raise all of the money that their company will ever need in one round. They are a few good reasons to try to do this.

1. Ensure that you'll have enough capital – fundraising in the future may be difficult, and
2. Avoid spending more time fundraising in the future.

There are, however, two key reasons to break your fundraise into tranches.

First and foremost, if your company needs a lot of capital over its lifetime, it may be difficult to assemble a syndicate of VCs willing to invest the target amount of capital. VCs typically have limits as to the size of their initial investment, meaning that to raise a sum that significantly exceeds those limits, you may need to seek capital from non-traditional early-stage investors. These investors often do not understand the venture model and fail to help startups reach their potential or raise money from venture investors.

The challenge with the latter option is that most VCs have target percentages of the company that they expect to own for their investment. As a result, if you try to create a syndicate with too many VCs, the structure will not work. Either the VCs will collectively own a lot of your company (leaving you with too little) or the VCs will not meet their target ownership levels and likely opt to not participate. Structuring a venture deal is a balancing act – taking anything to the extreme rarely works.

The second reason that pursuing a multi-round fundraising strategy may help you is because it may enable you to own more of the company. Simply put, capital raised when the company is more mature will likely be raised at a larger valuation, meaning that your stake is diluted less by each additional dollar that you raise.

THE IDEAL TIMES TO RAISE CAPITAL IN THE LIFE CYCLE OF A FUND

In theory, VCs have the same standards for making investments at any point in time. However, I believe that this does not hold true in practice.

VCs take into consideration the context in which each investment is made. For example, if the fund is performing poorly, they may increase their standards of investment, leading to longer diligence periods and a higher propensity to say no. However, if the fund is already doing very well, VCs might be

HOW MUCH TO SAY YOU ARE RAISING

As aforementioned, both entrepreneurs and VCs face conflicting incentives in determining how much capital the company should raise. Good VCs know that once they have made an investment in the company, they are on the entrepreneur's team and therefore want the company to succeed, which means helping the entrepreneur raise the right number.

There is another consideration that entrepreneurs need to engage: How much should they tell the VC they are raising, when asked. There is no right answer to the question, but there are a couple of dynamics of which to be aware.

The number that you quote may be different from what you actually raise. As you begin to work more closely with VCs, they may advise you to take more or less depending on the needs of your company. VCs are aware of this dynamic and aren't going to hold you to the exact number that you quote. So don't feel too much pressure when you give this answer – you're not going to shoot yourself in the foot.

However, you should try to give your best answer to this question. You could frustrate the VC and embarrass yourself a bit if you are off by an order of magnitude. It looks bad if you say you are raising $50 million when you only need $5 million.

The next dynamic to consider is that VCs understand that there is rarely one answer to this question. With more money, you will be able to increase your headcount or expand your marketing budget. It can be difficult to find the balance that positions the company for success and has acceptable implications for all parties involved. Again, a good VC should help you navigate this balancing act.

Given these dynamics, I think the best answer to this question is a range. Offer a low number that is enough to enable the business get to the next round of funding, and a high number that will help the company more rapidly achieve its short-term goals. Be prepared to tell the VC what you plan to do with each level of investment – so they can understand the differences in the scenarios (e.g., more sales people, etc.).

Offering a range is the best answer for a few reasons:

1. It helps the VC understand how money can drive growth in the company.
2. It demonstrates how thoughtful you are being about how to operate and finance the company.
3. It signals to the VC that you are going to be a flexible partner who is

willing to work toward the solutions that are best for the company.

4. It's a lot easier for you to create some reasonable scenarios than it is to definitively decide the optimal amount of capital for your company.

HIGH VALUATIONS CAN PUT ENTREPRENEURS AT RISK

People always want to get the best deal they can. For entrepreneurs, this typically means getting the highest valuation when raising money. The higher the valuation, the less of the company the entrepreneur will sell to VCs when taking an investment.

Like all things in life, however, moderation is key. Entrepreneurs who succeed in obtaining extraordinarily high valuations can risk their own financial rewards; there are three problems that excessively high valuations can create.

First, inflated valuations can limit the company's access to short-term resources. By maximizing the valuation, an entrepreneur may only attract dumb money and lose access to the credibility and resources offered by the most sophisticated VCs for the current round.

Second, as the valuation increases it is likely that fewer investors will be willing to invest in the future. If the valuation continues to increase after each round, entrepreneurs may find that there are no other investors willing to get involved, leaving them with the challenge of trying to milk existing investors, reduce costs or consider reducing their valuation.

Reducing the valuation of the company in the future can be painful for the entrepreneur as they may lose a significant portion of their equity. This happens because many investors use anti-dilution provisions to protect themselves. These legal terms allow investors to partially protect their equity stakes in the event of future investment rounds being completed at reduced valuations (also known as down rounds). Ultimately, in a down round the ownership of the current equity holders declines. These anti-dilution provisions leave the entrepreneurs to bear the brunt of this dilution. This protects the investor from the consequences of entrepreneurs who don't perform well or over-value their company early on. Since these terms are commonplace, entrepreneurs have an incentive to value their company appropriately to ensure that future valuations continue to increase.

In sum, it rarely pays to be greedy. While some succeed in over-valuing their companies, cutting aggressive deals can come back to haunt them as sophisticated investors know how to protect themselves from overstated valuations. In the end, it seems that it's always better to do deals that value your company reasonably.

have a falling out early in the company's life, while in other situations, founders realize that there isn't a clear need for their skill set in the company going forward, or they decide that they want to pursue a different career path.

A founder's decision to pursue other activities can be a signal to investors that they don't believe in the merits of the startup, but this does not necessarily prevent the remaining founders from raising capital. As long as there is an acceptable reason for the founder's defection, investors will likely evaluate the opportunity based upon the merits of the remaining founders & management team. Ultimately, investors are generally focused on who will be leading the company going forward.

HOW DEVELOPED DOES YOUR MANAGEMENT TEAM NEED TO BE?

The management team is very important to VCs. Few VCs making Series A investments don't want to take management risk, or the risk that the company will not have a strong founding management team, when they make their initial investment. They expect the best entrepreneurs to attract talented partners to their venture before seeking funding.

However, some seed investors (which include high-net-worth investors and a select group of VCs) are willing to take some management risk when they make their investments. As a VC I have made seed investments in companies that inevitably did not have a complete management team. That said, there is an important distinction here – while we didn't expect the whole team to be in place, we required the existing managers to be excellent, ensuring that the company had a strong founding team. In point of fact, most Series A investors, myself included, do not expect a full management team to be in place, but most of the key members should be on board by the time you seek a Series A. Most seed investors will be more forgiving on this issue. As a result, if you have the DNA of a founding CEO, you might be able to raise a seed round without having yet built out your team.

As for outsourcing, you can outsource some of the functions, but not the jobs. In the very early stages (pre-launch) of a company, you may not need a full time CFO. A financially savvy team member or a consultant can fill in some of the functions of a CFO, COO, SVP of Sales or other. However, as you begin to scale the operation it is important to add people to the team who can specialize in functional areas. The one-man team model doesn't scale well. As more customers need to be served, more analysis needs to be done, more new hires need to be trained and so on, the one-man (or otherwise understaffed) team model is hazardous. It ensures that nothing is done well. For a business to grow at a pace that seed or later round investors will get excited about, you need to build out a team quickly, and that starts with a core group of senior members.

THE SIGNIFICANCE OF GRAY HAIR

One reader of my blog asked whether VCs think talented young entrepreneurs are sufficiently qualified managers. It depends.

VCs frequently take meetings with less experienced entrepreneurs and they often invest in them. Experience is not inherently a barrier. Nobody assumes that being less experienced makes you incapable of building substantial value. What some entrepreneurs lack in experience, they more than make up for in hunger, creativity, intelligence and drive.

Young entrepreneurs are valued. VCs expect them to have unique drive and commitment to their ideas that can improve the odds of success. This energy factor can go a long way in some aspects of the business, including product design, inspiring employees and grabbing lots of media attention.

However, some companies are more complex, requiring management to develop large organizations, enterprise sales functions and other more technical business components. In most cases, theses initiatives are more successful when someone with deep experience leads the charge.

As a result, the answer to this question is a function of what the business intends to accomplish. If there are business units that require substantial experience, a team of young guns isn't going to be sufficient.

The key to success for less experienced entrepreneurs lies in understanding that they don't know what they don't know. Being wise enough to seek help is a critical component of success. The takeaway from this is that entrepreneurs should do their best to objectively evaluate the needs of their company and make a best effort to put the right team together, regardless of age.

Your Process

WHEN TO RAISE VENTURE CAPITAL

Timing the raise of your first venture round is an important consideration. I have heard some argue that if you try to raise VC too early, you can leave investors with a bad taste in their mouths and an unwillingness to consider your company again in the future. If you wait too long to start your raise, your company could go bankrupt, you may need to make salary cuts that cause you to lose key employees or your competitors may have an improved chance to grab market share before you.

The conventional answer to this question is a good one: "Raise money when you can." Capital markets can dry up, competitors can lock up investments from VCs before you knock on their doors and other opportunities can steal the attention of the investment community. While there are exceptions to every rule, the longer you wait to start the fundraising process, the wider the window generally is for exogenous factors to impact your chances for success in that process. Furthermore, socializing your concept with a VC early in the company's development can be an effective way to demonstrate the competency of the management team.

You should be aware, however, that your company is not likely to receive funding unless it has met the milestones that are typical for each stage of a company's funding lifecycle. You should be sure to approach investors who invest at your stage.

In sum, there are a lot of stars that need align in order for your company to raise capital. If a window to raise capital presents itself, you probably should jump through it.

DO YOU NEED TO QUIT YOUR DAY JOB?

It's relatively common for an entrepreneur to start working on a new venture while still employed by another company. A few entrepreneurs have asked me if it's acceptable to start raising a seed round while still keeping a day job.

The answer to this varies by firm, investor and startup. In general, this is a strike against the entrepreneur as it signals to investors that the entrepreneur is not extremely confident about the prospects of the endeavor. However, investors understand that you might have a mortgage to pay and kids to feed, and don't always hold it against you.

While VCs see these situations often, a good excuse is usually helpful. Be prepared to offer a strong explanation for why you haven't made the leap to going full time. You should also emphasize that you and your team will become full time upon receiving an investment.

If you need to maintain a job while you start your company, do it. At the end of the day, if you can work double time, make progress and demonstrate your competency while collecting paychecks, you should still be positioned to raise your initial capital.

TOP TEN LIST: HOW THE BEST ENTREPRENEURS INTERACT WITH VCS

Now to turn the tables, I will offer some thoughts about the best practices for entrepreneurs.

While the following list is not complete, perfect or without exception, these ten rules should serve as strong guidelines for entrepreneurs who want to create enduring relationships with VCs.

1. Only contact VCs who invest in your type of company (e.g., sector, stage, etc.): Living by this rule will save you time and prevent you from looking clueless.

2. Be honest about your intentions: I'm a firm believer that the best approach to business is the honest one. Be up front with your potential investors about your expectations, needs and level of interest in them.

3. Be patient with VCs: VCs are extremely busy and therefore your patience with them is appreciated. No, this isn't a cry for pity – it's just the nature of the job. While a busy schedule isn't an excuse (in my opinion) for not responding to appropriate emails, it does suggest that a bit more patience than average is warranted.

4. Actively share information: It is important to maintain momentum with investors to keep them interested. In order to do this you should openly provide information (you are comfortable disclosing) about your company and respond quickly to requests.

5. Do not take rejection personally: There are a lot of reasons why you might not receive funding from a VC – some of which are entirely unrelated to your company. As a result, you shouldn't take it personally. Don't let a rejection affect your ego.

6. Do not harass VCs (they're people too): Enough said.

7. Focus on the success of the company; check your ego at the door: This point should work both ways; both VCs and entrepreneurs should focus on making decisions that maximize shareholder value.

8. Be open to feedback and new ideas: Enough said.

9. Do not sully the reputation of a VC simply because you did not like their decision: Bad karma has a way of making its way back to its

creator. It's a small world and VCs talk to each other. Seeking undue vengeance can create challenges for entrepreneurs in their current and future fundraising efforts.

10. Build relationships with VCs: It seems to me that the greatest entre-preneurs are capable of getting past the business side of the relationship with a VC and engaging them on a more personal level. Developing a personal relationship with a VC can make the fundraising process significantly easier and more enjoyable.

PICKING THE VCS

Finding the Fit

NOT ALL VCS ARE CREATED EQUAL

There are four ways a VC adds value to a startup: capital, advice, contacts and credibility.

Capital is a relative commodity – any VC who keeps the proper reserves for each portfolio company does this well. One VC's money is not more green than another's. It is, however, important to think about how much capital each VC has available to support your venture through its future financial needs. I cover this in more detail below.

Often, the bigger differentiators come in from the VC's ability to provide useful advice, contacts and credibility. In my opinion, entrepreneurs can typically assess a VC's ability to deliver value by reading the bios of the founders. Impressive teams, more often than not, add a lot of value to their portfolio companies. Teams with a lot of experience can offer useful advice. Teams with high caliber credentials often have the opportunity to build a large and useful Rolodex. Teams that had success in business can transfer their credibility to their portfolio companies – an investment can be a sign of validation.

In examining the experience of a VC team, consider both their pre-VC experience and the companies they have backed as venture investors. If you receive a term sheet from a VC, consider doing deeper diligence on the team by contacting the CEOs of previous and existing portfolio companies.

I believe that the quality of a fund's team is the best indicator of the value that they will add, but there are other types of strategic value that a fund can offer, such as unique contacts (to government entities or particular types of companies) or unique access to capital. There are many funds that do not offer anything beyond the basic four types of value add mentioned above. Entrepreneurs should be sure to evaluate both the competency of the venture fund's team and the unique resources that they can bring to the table.

Entrepreneurs don't always have a choice when it comes to picking their VC backers. However, when they do, it's important to pick a venture fund that can most effectively help their business grow.

UNDERSTANDING A VC'S THESIS

It is very important to understand a VC's thesis when deciding whether or not to engage them in the fundraising process. Engaging a VC who doesn't invest in your sector, stage or geography can be a waste of both their time and your time.

I do want to note that, while you should only reach out to VCs for whom your business is a potential fit, you should be careful not to eliminate VCs that are a near fit before you have reached out to them. There are two reasons for maintaining this flexibility: 1) VCs make exceptions and invest slightly outside of their theses for the right opportunities, and 2) each call or meeting with a VC can help you polish your presentation, generate advice and open new doors to partners or other investors, etc.

Nonetheless, here are some tactics for better understanding a VC's thesis:

- Review the description of the VC's investment focus on their website (although do note that VC websites typically are not very informative about the nuances of their thesis). While the information on the website may be a bit vague, it typically will give some parameters about preferred investment size, sector and geography.
- Look through their portfolio (also on the website in nearly every case) - that should give you a sense of the sectors and geographies in which they invest.

- Read third party websites.
- Ask around in the community.

WHY VC WEBSITES STINK

The first source you should use to learn about a venture fund it the venture funds' website. Unfortunately, most VC websites stink – they provide very little information. To be honest, this is a phenomenon that I don't fully understand. However, I will do my best to rationalize it.

First, regarding to the poor aesthetics of the sites, I am sure part of the story is tied to laziness or cheapness. However, I think that there might be a bit more here. VCs play matchmaker between conservative Wall Street money and the cutting-edge future of our society. My intuition tells me that some VCs keep their websites conservative in order to show the right face to their investors.

The second issue with VC websites relates to their description of their investment strategy. I have found that VCs who share a sector and stage often have nearly identical descriptions of their investment strategy. However, when you talk to them they focus on different sectors, prefer different types of barriers to entry and seek different types of management. There strategies can also diverge when it comes to an underlying philosophy that drives investment decisions.

Unfortunately, few of the nuances that differentiate them are captured (or even highlighted) on their websites. My best guess as to why VCs do this is because they want to cast a wide net. I suspect that they don't want to be too specific and scare away an opportunity that might be slightly adjacent to their investment strategy, but an opportunity that they want to invest in nonetheless.

This certainly puts entrepreneurs at a disadvantage when trying to find VCs who have strategies that align with their ventures. As a result, entrepreneurs should be sure to speak to other founders, VCs and agents to get a better sense of the VC landscape.

Maybe someone will create a robust set of categories that describe VCs investment strategies so that there is a relatively common lexicon for evaluating what VCs invest in. However, until then keep hoping that the next generation of VCs will do a better job with their websites.

THE ADVANTAGES OF A LOCAL VC

When you are selecting VCs to target in your first fundraising process, their office location(s) should be a key consideration.

VCs whom you expect to serve as your key advisors should be located close to your offices. Proximity makes them accessible, enabling you to meet with them for advice more often. Additionally, local VCs are likely to be able to attend more board meetings in person, because they don't have to spend as much time commuting.

Aside from your core advisors, you should consider targeting VCs with deep networks in key regional industries. For example, if you are starting a new media company in Denver, you may want a New York VC on your board who can open doors on Madison Avenue.

In sum, be strategic when targeting VCs. By aligning the geography of your venture investors, you will get more value from the relationship.

CONSIDER AVAILABLE CAPITAL WHEN SELECTING VCS

It is important to consider a VC's available capital when deciding whether to contact them. Most VCs advertise their assets under management (AUM) on their website. However, it is worthwhile to note that while AUM is a decent indicator of capital that will be available to your firm, it is not the best metric. There are a few reasons for this. First, the AUM metric includes assets that have already been invested. A VC who just finished investing a fund (and has not yet raised another) may not have any available capital to invest despite having a large AUM number listed on their website.

While VCs with more capital under management are more likely to be able to support your company through subsequent rounds of funding, the three metrics that you should pay attention to are:

1. The amount of un-invested capital,
2. The capital reserves for each portfolio company and
3. The AUM per investment professional.

Generally, VCs who have a significant amount of un-invested capital are going to feel comfortable putting more capital into your company now and in the future. There certainly are a number of exceptions to this rule, but this metric can serve as reasonable high-level guidance on how easy it will be for the VC to continue to support your company in the future.

The second consideration is the target amount of capital deployed to each company. The amount of capital saved for future rounds of investment in a portfolio company is called a "capital reserve."

Generally, VCs with larger funds deploy more capital to each investment, over the lifetime of the company. However, this is not always the case – some larger funds seek to invest in more companies, keeping invested dollars per company down. As a result, you need to ask each firm what type of reserves they keep (if they don't explicitly state it on their website).

The third factor to consider is the business needs of funds that have a large ratio of AUM to investment professionals, as these funds may have incentives to act in a manner that is sub-optimal for the entrepreneur. Since most VCs only have the time to make a relatively fixed number of good investments, when this ratio is higher, VCs need to invest more capital in each company.

This can create two challenges for entrepreneurs. First, many VCs with a high ratio of AUM to investment professionals try to avoid syndicating investments, as they want to provide all of the capital for each round. While this means the entrepreneur won't have to spend time pitching to syndicate VCs, it does mean that entrepreneurs will not realize the benefit of having another VC invested in the company. Having more VCs involved usually means access to more knowledge, contacts and experience. More VCs also means a greater chance of receiving additional investment when (and it usually happens) the company encounters an obstacle that requires more cash than it has in its coffers to overcome.

The second concern with funds that have a high ratio of AUM to investment professionals is that they may try to force capital on entrepreneurs when the company does not need the money. These VCs have a strong incentive to invest more capital and this incentive may not always align with the best interest of the company.

Ideally, you should evaluate VCs on these metrics. If, in the end, you have the choice of several investment partners, this information can prove to be very useful.

TYPES OF RISKS VCS TAKE

Different VCs take different types of risks. When you are selecting VC funds to target, be sure to avoid funds that do not take risks associated with your venture.

The risk categories essentially can be organized according to the investment criteria that VCs consider. While there are many risks associated with any investment, I will include a short list of risks that typically distinguish one VC investor from another.

- **Management risk:** While few VCs will state that they are willing to gamble on a bad management team, some VCs place more importance on the strength of the management team than others. Some believe that an average team can make money with a good idea, others don't.

- **Product risk:** Commonly referred to as technology risk in the IT sector, product risk refers to the chance that the product will not be successfully developed. If your product is a highly complex piece of software that has not yet been developed, you are asking a VC to gamble on your team's ability to get the coding done with a given set of resources. Some VCs will take that risk, and others won't.

- **Revenue model risk:** Revenue risk refers to the potential that your company may not have a model for generating revenue. Not every business plan includes a revenue model and some that do don't have very good ones. Some VCs are comfortable backing the YouTubes of the world – ideas that will attract lots of users – with the belief that the entrepreneur will figure out how to monetize the service later. Others want to see a plan for generating revenue up front.

- **Market risk:** Market risk refers to the risk that the addressable market may not exist. Truly disruptive technologies rely on an assumption of adoption, which may not materialize. Furthermore, markets may dissolve if the landscape undergoes unforeseen change. Some VCs require that the market be validated through customer adoption; others don't.

- **Competitive risk:** Competitive risk refers to the potential for a venture to be beaten to market, outperformed or substituted. Competitive risk varies by the competitive landscape, barriers to entry, threat of new entrants and so on. VCs' aversion to this risk varies.

- **Partnership risk:** Partnership risk refers to the risk that key partnerships may not be obtained. This significance of this risk is driven by the importance of the partnership to the success of the business, the number of potential partners and the difficulty of obtaining partnerships. As with the other risks, VC tolerance for this varies greatly.

You should honestly evaluate each category of your business when selecting VCs to target. Your time will be better spent if you only pursue VC funds that can accept the risks associated with your business.

Unfortunately, most VCs do not articulate their risk profiles on their websites. The best way to learn about a VC's appetite for specific risks before using a favor to get introduced is to both look at their portfolio and ask around.

Implications of How a VC is Funded

HOW VCS ARE FUNDED

VCs typically get the money they invest to entrepreneurs from four sources.

1. **Diverse LPs:** The most common funding source comes from a diverse group of limited partners (e.g., university endowments, high net worth individuals, insurance companies and pension funds).

2. **Family office:** The second most common source of capital is from one limited partner, typically an extraordinarily wealthy family or corporation.

3. **Public markets:** VCs also raise capital by becoming publicly traded companies. Shares are purchased on the open market, giving the VC fund capital to invest.

4. **Government:** Some VCs are part of a state or local government, investing money with the objective of generating returns and enhancing the local economy.

The way a VC is funded affects how the fund will be invested. I will go into each category in detail to discuss the implications for the entrepreneur.

DIVERSE LPS

Investments made in a VC fund by a diverse group of limited partners are integrated in closed-end funds. As a result, VCs who raise money from a diverse group of LPs have to go and raise capital from limited partners every three to five years. Money is raised, the fund is closed, the capital is invested and then another fund is raised.

Entrepreneurs can be affected by the current fund's lifecycle. If you receive an investment from a VC when they are raising another fund, the VC will likely be slightly busier than they would be otherwise. Fundraising is a very time-consuming process for VCs. This doesn't mean that they won't have time for you, it just means that their schedules will be more complex and they will be slightly harder to reach.

However, this does not mean that they will not be able to make follow-on investments in your company. Good VCs keep capital reserves to support their portfolio companies even after they raise their next fund. Be sure to ask them about their reserve policy to ensure that they will be able to continue to support you.

Another consideration created by this funding structure is that these VCs often have a deeper network of people vested in your company's success. High-net-worth individuals who invested in the fund will care about the success of your company. If a VC has an investor (limited partner) who could help your company, they will typically contact them.

If someone raises money for a VC fund that performs poorly, they may not be able to raise a subsequent fund. As a result, in extreme circumstances they may be forced to find new jobs before you have sold your company.

FAMILY OFFICE

By "family office," I am referring to one family's private capital. In this scenario, the VC firm is essentially working for a very wealthy family to enhance the family's personal endowment.

Some of these VC funds can have a relatively limited amount of capital under management. Since they typically don't raise capital from third parties, they can only invest what the family allocated to them. Furthermore, once that's invested, they have to wait for a company to be sold in order to have access to more capital.

One risk is that if the fund invested a large proportion of assets under management, they may not have the resources to continue to support your company in future rounds. The takeaway is that you should look at their balance sheets before accepting an investment.

There is some risk that families may be able to pull their capital out of the fund if they have a sudden need for liquidity. The impact of this would again be an inability of the fund to support you in future rounds.

This is a question worth asking the VCs – they may or may not have protective provisions in their contract with the family that would prevent sudden withdrawals.

The psychology and objectives of a VC at a fund with fragmented LPs typically changes through the stages of their investment cycle; they are willing to take more risks at different points in the fund. While this is may be a pro and a con for the entrepreneur, it differs based on the styles of family office VCs.

Family office VCs with pools of capital that far exceed their investment capacity are more likely to have a consistent risk tolerance, making for more predictable investment decision-making. However, funds with more limited

AUM may become more risk adverse as capital pools continue to become increasingly constrained.

As I mentioned, VCs who have a fragmented limited partner base become very busy every three to five years as they go out to raise capital from their LPs. This can make them less accessible to their portfolio companies. However, the best ones make sure that they are still available.

Alternatively, family office VCs don't have to spend lots of time raising money, meaning they should be more consistently available to their entrepreneurs.

PUBLIC MARKETS

Similar to family office VCs, public funded VCs raise a relatively fixed pool of capital from public markets, which they continue to recycle from exits into new investments. Entrepreneurs should be sure to ask any fund that relies on recycled capital for future investments about their reserves to ensure that capital will be available in the future. In theory the fund can always tap the public markets, but that may not be the reality.

Public companies have to make public disclosures. As a result, more about your company and its operations may be easily accessible to third parties if you have a public investor. If your company requires substantial privacy because your strategy relies on being the first mover or otherwise, you should ask these VCs about the disclosures they will make.

To many entrepreneurs, bureaucracy is the antichrist. If this is the case for you, be aware of the additional administrative burdens that might be required if you accept money from a public fund.

These funds are regulated by the SEC and have substantial reporting requirements. Be prepared to answer questions and provide lots of data as necessary.

GOVERNMENT

Both the federal and local governments have created venture funds that seek to harness the free markets to achieve a social objective. The federal government has one fund that seeks to identify and incorporate new technologies into the military. Many state and city governments use these entities to stimulate local economies.

Similar to both the family office and public funds, these funds recycle capital from one investment to the next. As a result, capital constraints can be an issue if they don't have robust capital reserves and timely exits from other portfolio companies.

Furthermore, these funds are subject to the whims of legislators. It's possible that your capital reserves could be re-appropriated to another state agency with a change of administration or policy.

As aforementioned, these funds typically invest both to increase the size of their capital pool and to achieve a social objective (e.g., supporting new technologies, creating tax revenue or decreasing unemployment). Therefore, you should be thoughtful about the motivations of these VCs. A prerequisite for investment may require moving the company to a new location or taking the time to license the product to the government.

TOP TEN LIST: HOW THE BEST VCS INTERACT WITH ENTREPRENEURS

When selecting VCs to target, you may notice that VCs take varying approaches to the business. Tactics and practices vary greatly and some are better than others. I believe it is worthwhile for entrepreneurs to be aware and it is my hope that these guidelines will set the bar for entrepreneurs' expectations.

There is more to the business than picking winners; the nuances of interacting with and supporting entrepreneurs are potentially more important. While I have found there to be dozens of small processes that are exemplary, the principles that make a VC effective and poised for long-term success can be boiled down to a top-10 list. Although exceptions always exist, these ten guidelines appear to be the guiding light for how the best VCs interact with entrepreneurs.

1. They're respectful of entrepreneurs.
2. Handle sensitive information carefully.
3. Are forthcoming if you are evaluating competitive opportunities.
4. Are honest about your intentions.
5. Respond as promptly as possible.
6. Help entrepreneurs when possible regardless of whether or not you intend to invest.
7. Ensure that entrepreneurs share in the upside.
8. Are active board members.
9. Pursue the exits that are best for everyone around the table.
10. Support the entrepreneurial community.

More broadly, these guidelines address three potential VC shortcomings commonly cited by entrepreneurs: arrogance, inconsiderate behavior and selfishness. The best VCs avoid these behaviors like the plague, and they do it for good reason. In the long run, it makes them more successful.

The all-stars of VC understand that the entrepreneurs are the stars of the startup show. This perspective keeps actions that could be perceived as arrogant in check. With this mindset, these VCs know that egos are unjustified and, very often, destructive. Simply being respectful can make life for entrepreneurs easier and can enable a type of board room collaboration that yields the most productive outcome.

As I mentioned, VCs needs to be considerate in order to develop the kind of reputation that attracts the best entrepreneurs. Being considerate means a few things. First, it means stating intentions up front. For example, VCs who are looking at multiple opportunities in an industry need to inform entrepreneurs of that fact. Second, responding to entrepreneur emails in a timely fashion is also important. Responsiveness is part of being a team player – fundraising is a stressful process that does not need to be complicated for no reason. Furthermore, responding to emails is the same courtesy afforded to nearly everyone in business – entrepreneurs deserve the same respect. I have found that a quick "no" is always appreciated – like everybody else, entrepreneurs want to know where they stand. Promptly responding isn't always easy for VCs when their email inboxes are being bombarded, but efforts to be responsive are appreciated.

Lastly, even when VCs don't plan to invest, trying to selflessly help entrepreneurs is a noble pursuit – this goodwill gesture not only helps a VC's reputation, it is the right thing to do. Helping an entrepreneur can increase the odds that a new service makes it to market, that new jobs are created and one person gets a little bit closer to realizing a dream.

The best VCs understand that being perceived as arrogant, inconsiderate and selfish can damage their reputation and future deal flow. As a result, they go to great lengths to avoid these perceptions. Ultimately, this unique alignment is one of my favorite aspects of the VC role – it's in a VC's best interest to be a good guy.

PREPARING YOUR MATERIALS

THE THREE KEY FUNDRAISING DOCUMENTS

There are a number of materials that you may need to provide to an investor during the course of the fundraising process. Three of these documents, however, are ones that nearly every investor will want to see, as they each play a critical role in the process of engaging the investor.

Executive Summary

The executive summary provides a very concise overview of your company, only including enough information to get the meeting. This document will not likely be used again with a particular investor once he or she is engaged.

PowerPoint Presentation

The PowerPoint presentation is a document you will use in numerous meetings with a given investor to describe your business in enough depth to get the investor interested in learning more. This document alone will not provide the investor with enough information to make a decision to invest, but it should provide an overview of the key facets of your business that will motivate him or her to dive deeper.

Note that some folks elect to use their presentation as an executive summary as well. In my opinion, it's better to have a separate Word document to get the first meeting.

The Operational Financial Model

After you have piqued the interest of venture capitalists, they will request a variety of diligence materials. One universal diligence item that will be included in that list is your financial model, an Excel document that quantitatively illustrates how you anticipate the business evolving. This model should provide investors with more than your financial projections – it should also illustrate how your operations evolve (e.g., when you plan to hire people and when you plan to spend money on marketing) enabling investors to understand the mechanics of the business. In sum, this document will explain how you plan to build the company.

The Bait

WHAT IS AN EXECUTIVE SUMMARY?

As I mentioned, a VC's objective in the first phase of the process is to simply determine if they want to learn more about your idea. To drill this home, they're not deciding if they want to invest; they're deciding if they want to meet you and hear the real pitch. Executive summaries should be aligned with this; they should only provide the information that is needed to pique a VC's interest.

At a high level, VCs assess businesses based upon a handful of key characteristics. As a result, an executive summary should provide this high-level information clearly and concisely. Providing too much detail at this point will likely get in the way.

Aside from basic contact information, an executive summary should include the following high-level information:

- The geographic location of your company
- A mission statement
- A product/service overview (including a description of the pain point that is addressed)

- An estimate of the addressable market
- An assessment of your company's competitive landscape
- A brief explanation of your barriers to entry
- A short list of achievements to date
- A summary of financials (historical and projected revenue, EBITDA and key metrics, such as volume)
- An overview of capital raised in the past and fundraising objectives for this round
- A list of objectives that you plan to achieve before the next fundraising round
- Short management bios

Surprisingly, most summaries fall short in describing their product or service. Make sure that this is very clear – "keep it simple stupid." Someone who knows nothing about your space should be able to understand it.

All of this should be one to two pages, single-spaced. Use section titles to help VCs quickly find the information they need. No fancy graphics or art is required.

The executive summary just needs to provide the high-level information required to help a VC figure out that he wants to learn more. Your chance to fill in the gaps will come later.

OVERVIEW OF FUNDING STATUS

Your executive summary should include a very short overview of your funding status. This section needs four pieces of information: how much you have raised to date, who made that investment (e.g., founders, angels), how much you are raising in this round and the very high-level intended uses of this capital (e.g., complete technology, increase sales staff). This section should be kept very brief, integrated into one to three sentences or a few bullet points.

If you're not exactly sure how much you are raising, put a range in the executive summary. This isn't an issue, as VCs understand that there are different scenarios – more or less staff, or a longer or shorter period before your next fundraising.

Do not put a valuation of the company in the executive summary. Including a pre- or post-money valuation can appear to be presumptuous, and if your expectations are too high it can make investors lose interest before your first meeting. Remember, the purpose of this document is to get a meeting, not close the whole deal.

It's good to be forthcoming about your financial requirements; investors are comfortable talking about money. Keep this section very simple and you'll be one step closer to landing a meeting.

COMPETITIVE LANDSCAPE OVERVIEW

In your executive summary, include a brief overview of your company's competitive positioning. At the very least this should be one sentence that might indicate anything from a "monopoly situation from …" (which could happen if you have a very significant barrier) to "differentiated by X, Y, Z."

What this bullet should not say is "no competition." Every company has competition, even if there isn't another company doing what you're doing. Cutting-edge innovators often face competition from the old way of doing things that they're trying to replace. For example, online real estate brokerages face competition from their brick and mortar counterparts. If you are truly an innovator in your market, be prepared to discuss how you are going to compete with the old business models you intend to displace.

NOTE THE MILESTONES BEFORE YOUR NEXT ROUND

One really smart entrepreneur sent me an executive summary that included a list of milestones they expected to achieve after closing this round of fundraising. I found this to be a valuable addition to the executive summary for a couple of reasons.

First, this section (which was no more than a few bullets) demonstrated that they understand the fundraising process, making me feel more comfortable with their ability to manage the fundraising side of the business going forward.

Second, this shed a little light on "how" they were thinking about building their company. By highlighting their next steps, I had a better understanding of how they prioritized operational initiatives.

Space is always tight in an executive summary, but if you can spare one line to rattle off what you intend to achieve with the capital you are raising (in order to prepare for your next round of funding) you will look even more sophisticated to investors.

EXECUTIVE SUMMARY MANAGEMENT BIOS

Your executive summary should include an overview of the management team. This section is your chance to let investors know that you have a talented team without taking too much space on the page.

I recommend that you start this section with a one-sentence overview of your team. This should mention how many people are on the team and their overall expertise. An easy way to sum up your expertise is to indicate the combined number of years of relevant experience that your team has.

After the one-sentence overview, include up to two- or three-sentence bios. The bios should paint a high-level picture of the individual's credentials. The first part of this bio should be an overview of each individual's work experience. This may take one or two sentences. For example, "Two-time entrepreneur; founder of company A (5x return)" or "10 years in retail industry. VP of merchandising at Clothing Co." The second part of the bio should be a listing of academic degrees.

If done properly, this section of the executive summary can quickly let VCs know that you are a competent group of professionals, giving them another reason to invite you in for a meeting. As most VCs will tell you, the quality, experience and likeability of the team are essential elements of any investment decision. So be sure to highlight your team's strengths.

POWERPOINT PRESENTATIONS ARE NOT EXECUTIVE SUMMARIES

At their first point of contact with a VC, many entrepreneurs send their PowerPoint presentations instead of an executive summary. This is a bad approach – PowerPoint presentations rarely function well as executive summaries

Most PowerPoint presentations are designed to be presented verbally (these are called "stand up" presentations). Consequently, they tend to have few words on each slide to avoid distracting the audience. However, because there is very little content on a good "stand up" presentation slide, these documents make for very bad executive summaries. All of the main insights that a presenter would traditionally say about the concept on each slide is absent when there's no one there to present them. Therefore, when VCs receive PowerPoint decks in lieu of a proper executive summary, they miss the important information that someone would be saying in the background. Usually, the message is lost. In a lot of cases, the slides don't have enough content to properly describe the product or service.

Also, PowerPoint presentations tend to be long, whereas executive summaries are short. With so many new plans to review each day, a VC is likely to give more attention to a document that they can digest in a few minutes.

In sum, be sure to send an executive summary that is in sentence and paragraph form. Otherwise, your chances of being asked in for a meeting will be decreased.

TOP 5 WAYS TO MAKE FUNDRAISING DOCUMENTS OPERATIONAL

VCs understand that the fundraising process is time consuming, taking entrepreneurs away from building the company. Creating documents for investors can be one of the most time-consuming parts of the process. While not all of the documents are likely to assist in operations, some of the materials can and should be created with operational purposes in mind to make the best use of these efforts.

Here are five ways to make the fundraising process more useful to your operation:

1. Create projections in a manner that makes them easy to use for future planning and budgeting.
2. Design your uses of capital raised analysis to play into your short-term budgets by making it sufficiently detailed.
3. Leverage the addressable market analysis to identify the most attractive target customer segments.
4. Revisit your competitive landscape when preparing investor materials to look for best practices and opportunities to enhance your model.
5. Generate a sales pipelines document that can be leveraged by your sales department going forward (you'll probably need an operational version of this document to share with your board in the future).

Fundraising can be a tedious process – try to get as much operational value out of it as possible.

THE IMPORTANCE OF GEOGRAPHY

Your executive summary should clearly list the location of your company's legal entity and physical headquarters because both of these factors are critical to many VCs' investment decisions. If the location of either of these is in flux, you should clearly indicate that fact in your executive summary.

VCs are thoughtful about which countries they will invest in as laws vary substantially. Lesser-developed judiciary systems generally present more risk for corporations and shareholders, adding significant gravity to decisions to invest abroad.

Furthermore, many VCs have told their investors (limited partners) that they will invest in specific geographies so that their limited partners can create a balanced portfolio, with the desired exposure to country-specific risks. VCs who want to keep their investors happy so they can raise money from these same investors in the future are compelled to make investments in geographies consistent with their stated theses.

That said, some VCs tell their limited partners that they will make investments in numerous regional or international geographies, positioning them to be flexible.

When you send a VC your executive summary, you should already know what geographies they will invest in and you should clearly indicate on your executive summary that your company is within the target geography. This will save VCs from having to ask you that question and make you look well prepared.

VCS APPRECIATE GEO-FLEXIBILITY

I was once asked if VCs prefer entrepreneurs who are willing to relocate their companies. VCs do use the location of a company as a selection criterion. VCs who only have capabilities in the US might not invest in a startup headquartered in China. Therefore, a founder's willingness to move his company into the VC's target geography can make the difference when the VC is deciding to invest.

There are, however, other considerations that should influence an entrepreneur's or VC's willingness to move or back a company that is moving, respectively. First, both investors and entrepreneurs should only be interested in moving the company if it does not disrupt the core business. If a swath of effective employees would have to be replaced, new partnerships forged or new customers acquired, investors might be averse to backing a company that is relocating.

Second, some VCs are hesitant to back entrepreneurs that don't have deep relationships in the local ecosystem. There's a rational argument for this – without a local network, finding talent and getting introduced to key contacts can be difficult.

Ultimately, the decision to back a startup that is changing locations is typically made on a case-by-case basis. When a move into a VC's target geography is beneficial for the company, however, it is generally looked upon favorably.

WHAT IS A MISSION STATEMENT?

When most people think of a mission statement, they think of some stodgy cluster of bullet points that state trite company values and objectives. When done poorly, these appear designed to falsely boost employee morale, pepper press releases and fill in white space on marketing collateral. Unfortunately, more often than not mission statements are shams and do very little to help the company. However, when done well, they are tremendously valuable.

A mission statement is a single phrase or sentence that encapsulates your company's unique objective.

Unique is a key word here. Mission statements are most effective when they focus on the unique solution that your company intends to provide. There are two reasons for this. First, including commonplace objectives such as becoming a large company or generating profits does not clarify what makes your company different. Second, they do not implicitly communicate the pain point that you intend to address.

Google has a great mission statement, "Google's mission is to organize the world's information and make it universally accessible and useful." It's clear what they are trying to achieve and the pain point is obvious: the world's information is currently highly inaccessible and useful. Big visions are the foundations of disruptive companies, so when someone hears your mission statement they should be able to understand what about the world you are going to change.

It's also critical that the mission statement focus on the "what," not the "how." The mission of eBay is "To provide a global trading platform where practically anyone can trade practically anything." In this one sentence, it's not critical to understand that they will leverage technology, hire marketing people or otherwise in order to do this.

Some companies confuse mottos and mission statements. Mottos are a summary of values that management hopes to superimpose on their staff. In my opinion, mottos generally come off as disingenuous. Here's a cheesy one: "Respect, Integrity, Communication and Excellence." That was Enron's.

THE BENEFITS OF MISSION STATEMENTS: THE PROCESS

Most entrepreneurs don't create mission statements for their companies. This happens for a few reasons. First, most mission statements that serve as examples to entrepreneurs are done poorly, making them ineffective and giving this exercises a bad rap. As a result, I find that lots of entrepreneurs choose not to create them, electing not to waste time on what appears to be a lame management tactic. Second, many entrepreneurs never think about creating them, especially when the management team is hyper-focused on creating a product, business plan or raising money.

In my opinion, not creating one is a huge mistake. Developing a clear mission early in the company's development is critical. There are a number of reasons for this.

First, the process of creating a mission statement is hugely beneficial to founders. Since it's typically difficult to write less than more, boiling your company's over-arching goal down to one sentence is a daunting and nuanced task and the exercise of doing so should help the founders get on the same page.

Second, the process of defining a mission will help managers determine whether or not the scope of their effort is too big (and unnecessarily competes with incumbents) or is too small (and doesn't capture the real market opportunity).

Third, if you find that your mission statement is to create a better version of something that's already being done, your company may not be differentiated enough to make it through the throws of being the small player going head to head with incumbents.

The process of creating a mission statement defines and clarifies your team's objective, giving your team a polestar around which they can build their entire strategy.

THE BENEFITS OF MISSION STATEMENTS: COMMUNICATION

Entrepreneurs without good mission statements often find it difficult to explain what they are trying to do, making it more challenging for them to do business. This is either because they have not developed a coherent vision of their over-arching objective or because they have not worked through the process of describing their objective simply. Strong mission statements enable startups to effectively communicate their vision to employees, partners and investors.

A clear mission statement sets the corporate polestar, making it easy for members of the staff to know what ultimate objective they are working towards. While mission statements are often too high level to serve a useful guide for day-to-day activities, they ensure a consistent long-term trajectory and demonstrate the management is working toward a common goal.

Well-constructed mission statements are often very intriguing, as they implicitly identify a large opportunity associated with a significant pain point. When used properly, these one-liners serve as the perfect first response to any potential partner or investor's question about what you do, making for an ideal start to an elevator pitch. They are the easy-to-understand hook that leaves the other person wanting to learn more.

Entrepreneurs without mission statements typically start their elevator pitches with the "how." For example, without a mission statement, the Google founders might have started their pitch by saying, "We're building an algorithm that calculates a ranking of pages based upon the interlinking between pages." However, by starting with the objective, their pitch might have been catchier. Here's what they might have said with a mission statement in place, "We're trying to organize the information on the Internet in a manner that makes it uniquely accessible to consumers."

While too many mission statements seem to be a trite technique, I believe that they serve as a useful communication tool that can inspire employees and catch the attention of investors.

VALUE PROPOSITION OR PAIN POINT: MAKE THE CASE

When pitching to a VC, it's not enough to say that your future customers want or even need your service. You have to assume that the people across the table know nothing about your space and don't have a sense for sentiments and dynamics in the industry. In order to get VCs to believe that there is a strong need for your new idea, you have to make the case.

When you articulate this, you need to keep in mind that most VCs want to invest in ideas that address a pain point. It's not enough for a service to be cool or just useful because it doesn't guarantee that enough people will adopt it – it needs to solve a problem. There needs to be some urgency. In reality, these are often two sides of the same coin – the difference between simply making life easier and addressing a pain point for a VC comes down to your presentation. Change "everyone is going to be psyched to use this" to "people are wasting time and losing functionality without this." Focus on the pain.

Usually you can make the case with a few metrics. The best types of metrics quantify the pain: the cost of not using the service. Put this in dollars and cents if you can. If not, use the next best metric – time, megabytes, etc. If you can't put a metric on the cost, use something more qualitative: survey results or analyst opinions, etc.

Just a few of these metrics can go a long way. They give VCs something they can understand, even as an industry outsider.

If you spend time preparing your case, you'll spend less time making it.

ADDRESSABLE MARKET: NOT MARKET SIZE

Too many entrepreneurs confuse their addressable market with their market size. It's rare that these two numbers are the same. Mixing them up can be a problem.

The market size is the total revenue generated in a particular segment of the economy. For example, the Internet advertising industry may be X billion dollars this year – the total amount of money spent on advertising on the web.

The addressable market is the total amount of revenue that your company could generate if it acquired every potential customer. The entire group of potential customers is often referred to as the addressable population.

The addressable market is unique to your narrow industry focus and therefore is often different from the high-level market size numbers that analysts

ADDRESSABLE MARKETS ARE BASED ON NET REVENUE

Not all revenue is created equally. This is especially true for companies that sell a product or service on behalf of another party. In these situations revenue can be calculated in two ways. There's the gross revenue, which includes the money that is paid back through to the primary service provider. And then there is the net revenue, which excludes revenues that are directly passed through to the underlying service provider.

The net revenue is the number that really drives the business and therefore it is the number that should be used in your addressable market calculations.

BARRIERS: GET THE STORY RIGHT

VCs want to know that your business can't easily be copied since they want to avoid intensely competitive markets. When this question comes up you need to be prepared to provide an honest answer – one that not only doesn't over sell, but also doesn't under sell your company's position.

There are lots of types of barriers to entry. The most commonly cited are trade secrets and patents, partnerships, economies of scale and first mover advantage. Despite being frequently mentioned, first mover advantage is not in itself a barrier; it is an opportunity to create barriers (e.g., partnerships, economies of scale, network economies) before others enter the market.

In the information technology space, information and technology are also key barriers. Some companies accumulate information that differentiates their service from new entrants. An example of this is eBay. Their auction listings make them a more valuable service than an auction site with nothing for sale. Without content, any new entrant will face the quandary of getting enough initial listings on the site to attract users, before those users provide listings. It's usually a bit of a Catch-22. This can make for a substantial barrier.

Your technology can also be a barrier if it will take competitors significant time or resources to engineer an equivalent product.

When asked about your company's barriers, be honest. Explain the real barriers that your model creates. However, be sure not to embellish. You're not going to trick VCs and the expectations of barriers may be lower than you expect. You have more to lose than gain by exaggerating. Most companies do not have a deterrent for all competition – that's the norm. VCs generally think that it's okay to have some competitive vulnerability, as long as you have a talented team and the right idea.

Barriers to entry are an important part of your pitch. Be thoughtful about the competitive dynamic, be ready to articulate your position and be honest.

THE SIGNIFICANCE OF PATENTS

When discussing their barriers to entry, many entrepreneurs cite pending patents. While obtaining patents can be worthwhile, many IT-focused VCs do not believe that patents alone create sufficient barriers.

There are two reasons for this. First, the US Patent and Trademark Office can take years to issue the patent you are pursuing. In our rapidly changing markets, a new entrant could emerge, dominate and exit the market before your patent is approved and legal action is possible. Furthermore, the market could evolve sufficiently to render the patent meaningless by the time it is granted.

Second, the costs of enforcing patents are high. In order to stop a competitor from infringing on a patent, your company will need to spend hundreds of thousands, if not millions, of dollars. That type of suit can distract management and absorb vital resources. Furthermore, VCs are aware that they will be paying for any suits that take place during the infancy of the company.

However, VCs do recognize the value of patents. Many VCs believe that patents present a deterrent to competitors and can be a valuable asset at the companies exit. That said, it is important for entrepreneurs to understand the limited importance that VCs place on patents in order to place the proper emphasis on these assets when they present their company's barriers.

PROJECTIONS: NOTHING TO STRESS ABOUT

Entrepreneurs often expect VCs to react adversely to the projections that they include in the executive summary and business plan. This expectation appears to give management teams a bit of anxiety because their projections at this early stage are based on a lot of assumptions.

The reality is that VCs don't put too much emphasis on your revenue and profit forecasts at this stage of the company. There's good reason for this – before a company has significant revenue, the projections are essentially an educated guess. VCs know this.

This doesn't mean that early stage VCs don't care about the future growth of the business – they do. However, they don't rely on your projections to evaluate growth. VCs evaluate growth prospects based on, among other things, the addressable market size and competitive positioning of the business. If the addressable market is huge, the company addresses a real pain point, and the business has a competitive advantage (and high barriers), VCs assume that the company has the potential to grow rapidly.

This also doesn't mean that VCs won't want to see projections. VCs are interested in projections for three reasons. First, they want to see that reasonable assumptions will lead to rapid growth, confirming expectations based on the addressable market, the value proposition and the competitive landscape. Second, they want to see the math behind your projections both to understand your revenue model and assess management's ability to logically think about the drivers of the business. Finally, the projections will give VCs a sense for your strategic plan (how you will build the company), enabling them to better evaluate your management capabilities.

Be prepared to talk about the key drivers and assumptions in your projections candidly. It's okay to admit that some numbers are estimates. Just do your best to have a good rationale for every number that you use, and try to be convincing that your team can make assumptions reality.

OPERATING TIMELINE

One tool to further demonstrate how thoughtful you are regarding the company building process is an operating timeline.

An operating timeline is a simple diagram that shows the steps involved in building your business. While there are a number of ways to design this illustration, either time or more generic phases (i.e., phase I, phase II) are depicted horizontally and key tasks are listed vertically over time. Some will use a more traditional Gantt chart, others will create their own schematic. Inevitably, these diagrams are too large to fit into an executive summary, leaving them to only be prominent in presentations delivered by entrepreneurs in their first meeting.

Note that selecting the appropriate level of granularity of action items listed on your operating timeline is an important consideration. By showing more detail about the next steps of creating your business, investors will be more able to understand your ability to execute. Too much detail, however, can be onerous and boring to investors. Typically, the right balance is to describe the broad brush strokes. For example, you might mention company formation as an action item rather than a laundry list of the steps in that process (e.g., setting up a bank account, incorporating, etc).

Selecting the appropriate timeframe to depict is also important. Shorter timeframes demonstrate a tactical understanding of your business; longer timeframes illustrate broader strategic thinking. Showing the operating plan for a short timeframe – three months, for example – will force you to provide more detail about what your team will be doing on a weekly or monthly basis (e.g., making key hires, initiating sales conversations, testing technology). Again, this should give the investors an understanding of your plan of action and ability to manage the company development process.

A longer timeframe of several years, for example, will highlight how your company will evolve. Listing the launch of a new service or product, the targeting of a new customer segment or penetration of a new geography will help investors understand the broader strategic vision.

Since the timeframes can substantially change the messaging, it is helpful to show both a longer timeframe and a shorter timeframe at different points in your presentation. Often the longer timeframe is either shown up front when the entrepreneur is first trying to get the investors up to speed on the business, or toward the end of the presentation as a mechanism for integrating the bigger picture opportunity down the road.

The ways in which this diagram is depicted vary substantially, but the purpose remains the same. By showing the steps involved in building your company, you can help investors understand that you have thought through the process of launching your business.

The Presentation

HOW TO MAKE A GOOD INVESTOR PRESENTATION

Every time you have a meeting with a venture capitalist, you should be prepared to present a stock PowerPoint presentation that explains your business. You will definitely be expected to deliver a PowerPoint presentation in your first meeting, and may be expected to present it again at future meetings, when pitching to new partners or diving deep into a particular topic covered by one of your slides.

To clarify, your executive summary is not an appropriate document for these meetings. The brevity of the executive summary makes it only suited for getting you the meeting, while the PowerPoint presentation is used to provide more information about your company in meetings thereafter.

While the PowerPoint presentation should address all of the same topics of the executive summary, there are differences between the two documents.

First, the PowerPoint should be largely graphical; whereas the executive summary should only include text. Graphics should be used wherever possible to communicate your message as these slides will most likely be delivered by you or your team, meaning that someone will be able to explain them. Too much text can distract investors from listening to you and your team, or even worse, lead them to ignore the slides altogether. Nobody bothers to read paragraphs projected on a wall.

Second, the PowerPoint slides should provide more depth about your business plan. Where the executive summary provided a brief sentence or set of bullet points describing the pain point, product or competition, the Power-Point presentation should provide more color. Use statistics, visuals or even several slides to provide investors with a deeper explanation of the dynamics surrounding your business. Be careful to not go overboard, however, as the typical slide deck is only 10 - 20 slides with some slides as backup.

Lastly, the slide deck should provide the dimension of your startup that was excluded from the executive summary: how you will build the business. In order to explain the how, you will likely need to describe the relevant business ecosystem, illustrating how your business strategically fits into the marketplace. You will also need to describe operational aspects of the business, such as how you will build your product (e.g., who will program or build it) and how you will sell it (e.g., a sales or marketing strategy and what are the details of the plan).

NARRATIVE: PRESENTATION CONNECTIVE TISSUE

The slide deck that you show to VCs in your meetings should do more than address the requisite topics. Your presentation should tell a story that helps investors understand why this is an attractive opportunity.

There are a few reasons why creating a narrative through your slides is important.

First, people (investors included) like stories – they're more engaging than a string of seemingly unrelated facts. When done well, stories incorporate elements of suspense, insight and even a climax. These rhetorical tools can be incorporated into the presentation to make the materials more exciting and engaging. This is very important, as conjuring up an emotional response (even if a subtle one) in your audience can help them become more engaged with your venture.

Second, when asked about your venture over cocktails, you probably already explain the opportunity in a narrative format – it's more natural. In my experience, when asked, most entrepreneurs deliver compelling stories about their business in a conversational format. When they're asked to deliver a set of business slides about the company, however, they lose their mojo. The excitement about the business is lost in facts and figures; the larger story is reduced to a collection of facts. Generally speaking, asking a founder to switch from a conversational overview of their company to a set of slides is like watching a right-handed pitcher start throwing lefty. It's unnatural.

There's good reason for this. Most entrepreneurs view a slide deck as a checklist – a series of topics they need to address in order to answer the most common investor questions. At its lowest level, this is what a presentation is supposed to do – answer key questions about the business. Unfortunately, checklists and narratives mix about as well as oil and water. Stories have rhythm, while checklists drone on like the dry ticking of a metronome.

Most entrepreneurs simply deliver the dry checklist and assume that the business fundamentals will speak for themselves (and they often do). But there is an opportunity to go beyond the checklist and give the presentation a heartbeat. This is done by creating a narrative. The narrative comes from the connective tissue carefully inserted between the items on the checklist. Either through additional slides, or more commonly, taglines, the narrative weaves the generic building blocks of an investor presentation into a story.

It's worth noting that in some cases, the story comes to life throughout the entire presentation while in other situations, the narrative sits in the first half of the presentation and the remaining items of the checklist come after the narrative (completing the checklist).

Weaving a narrative into your presentation is of critical importance. It will bring your story to life, allow you to illustrate the enthusiasm that you have for your company and help to captivate investors.

THE INVESTMENT OVERVIEW SLIDE

There are lots of one-size-fits-all strategies for pitching VCs. I have heard of everything from using consulting frameworks (e.g., the four P's) to the Fabulous 14. I have found there to be a few weaknesses for these presentation strategies.

The problem is, I've been in few meetings where an entrepreneur has been able to run through the presentation from start to finish. Frankly, it's rare for many slides to be viewed at all, and even more rare for them to be viewed in order. There's a good reason for this – VCs are constrained by time, so they need to be efficient and get the answers they need in a very short meeting.

All of this chaos is confounded by the fact that VCs often don't give structure to the beginning of the meeting, enabling entrepreneurs to put their best pitch forward. Some entrepreneurs start with the impression that they will get to run through their whole pitch; however, it's not long before the VC pulls them in a new direction. If the entrepreneur was telling a multi-slide story, they may never reach the punch line.

There is not a single format that will work universally, but there is one tactic that can help. I recommend that you start the pitch with an investment over-view slide – a single slide with short bullet points that addresses key questions that a VC is bound to have about any investment. Include the following topics:

- Value proposition/pain point
- Addressable market size
- Barriers
- Competition
- Major achievements to date
- Management
- Overview of funding status

For each topic, include a very concise (one- to four-word) description of your venture. For example, write "Addressable Market: $1B" or Barriers: Patent, Network Economies."

These buzz words will create excitement and facilitate the conversation, ensuring that the VC will ask about all of the key elements of your business.

This slide has several benefits:

1. It enables you to informally provide an agenda for the meeting – since you will be asked to provide more detail about each category on the slide.
2. It allows you to get even the most rushed VCs interested early in the meeting before they take the conversation down one narrow tangent.
3. It shows the VCs that you understand their point of view – that you get it. This informally makes the case that you are a good management team.

Even with this investment overview slide, you should still have all detailed slides you might need at your disposal. You may only talk through the investment overview slide and a demo, or you may end up presenting every slide that you created. Either way, better safe than sorry.

I don't believe that one size fits all, but this one slide is likely to fit most.

ILLUSTRATING THE TEAM

In my experience, the team overview slide in the average entrepreneur's presentation is often the least effective. There's good reason for this – cramming a high-level overview of two to four backgrounds into a series of bullets nearly always results in a word wall. A word wall is a slide that has so many words on it that it looks more like a page of an essay than a slide. That format doesn't work well for presentations – nobody wants to read an essay when they're listening to a presentation.

So how do you show off your team's accolades without overloading a slide with text? You show, not tell.

I recommend that you use the following format for your team slides. Next to each team member's photo, put their name, title and tagline. The tagline should be a slightly fun 2 - 3 word description of that person's story. Some examples:

- "Serial entrepreneur"
- "UX guru"
- "Machine learning thought leader"

You get the idea. Below the tag for each person you should include a few academic or work-related logos that represent the experience of the person. While the logos won't explain everything that each person did at that institution, it will brand their experience with investors and queue up conversations about their experience. If your investors want more information about the team, they'll ask and you can tell them or send them follow up information. In the meantime, by putting less on the page, investors will digest more.

MAJOR ACHIEVEMENTS

On your investment overview slide you should provide a very concise overview of what you have achieved to date. Common achievements include: completion of stages of product development, recruitment of key team members, development of key partnerships, financial performance landmarks (e.g., first revenue) and acquisition of capital (e.g., angel, bridge loans, etc.).

This is your chance to brag. Just keep it short and sweet and it will go over well.

SUBSTANCE TRUMPS FORM, BUT FORM DOES MATTER

On occasion, entrepreneurs have asked whether it's more important to have nice-looking presentation materials or to have the right information in them. I think about it this way: It is my hope as an investor to never invest in a company that has a bad idea but pretty materials. Substance always trumps form.

This doesn't mean, however, that an entrepreneur shouldn't bother to make their presentation materials look acceptable (if not better). While I hate the idea of requiring entrepreneurs to spend more time than necessary in the fundraising process, there is value in having nice-looking documents.

A well-formatted executive summary and a nicely designed PowerPoint presentation do make a good impression. While I shouldn't care about the superficial aspects of a presentation, buttoned up materials are one signal that the entrepreneur has their act together.

Whether investors realize it or not, this likely has a small impact on decision making. Take the inverse, for example. If I'm being honest, when I see an executive summary that looks like a fifth grader made it, a little part of my psyche assumes that the management team isn't sophisticated or is just really lazy. While I consciously try to focus on the content in order to assess the opportunity, messy materials are a small strike against the entrepreneur.

The last reason I believe that form is an important signal is that the materials an entrepreneur sends an investor are likely to look a lot like the materials an entrepreneur would send a prospective partner or customer. If they can't put forward a professional foot with me, I can't be certain that they will do so with business contacts who are more likely to care about the state of the materials they receive.

CLIPART WON'T DO INNOVATIVE IDEAS JUSTICE

Putting forward a well-designed PowerPoint presentation demonstrates your ability to communicate in the business world, an important skill set for entrepreneurs who will have to present to future investors, partners and customers.

There is another reason to prepare a good-looking presentation: Your slides make an impression. Even if your business plan is cutting-edge and you communicate the concepts clearly, making those points with slides that use old clipart may leave investors with a not-so-innovative perception of your idea. The look and feel of your slides will shade an investor's perspective of your concept.

Furthermore, the design of the slides also impacts an investor's perception of you, the entrepreneur. There's good reason for this – the style of slides often reflects the temperament and character of the person who prepared them. Similar to comparing a master to his pet, zany entrepreneurs typically have zany slides, structured entrepreneurs have structured slides and sales-y entrepreneurs typically have sales-y slides. You get the idea. So showing dowdy old clip-art-based slides won't make you look very cutting-edge.

A basic rule to follow with creating slides is that if you can't find the right image, don't include one. Draw a diagram or find some other visual, but don't settle for clipart.

TRENDY TERMS DON'T MAKE YOUR COMPANY INNOVATIVE

Every couple of years or so, a thought leader will coin a new phrase for a business trend. Web 2.0, the longtail and others have all been part of this trend.

While these terms help us describe new aspects of our business landscape, entrepreneurs should be careful in how they use these words when pitching investors.

Especially when terms are new, not well-understood or fully defined, it's wise for entrepreneurs to be reticent in labeling their business with a recently-coined term. While your company may in fact be part of the new trend in business, explicitly taking ownership of a new label is like calling your business "innovative." When investors hear you say that your company is innovative they will likely do an internal eye-roll; be more focused on determining whether or not you were justified in making that claim. Rather, when pitching investors, you're better off focusing on explaining the fundamentals of your business. If your company is in fact innovative, it will become self-evident.

Similarly, if your company is part of a cutting-edge trend, it's typically better to let the plan speak for itself than try to brand it as a coined term.

IT'S DANGEROUS TO CALL YOUR COMPANY "THE GOOGLE OF _____"

It's common for entrepreneurs to compare their new ideas to existing companies. There is good reason for this – the easiest way to describe a concept is often to reference commonplaces such as well-known companies with similar characteristics.

While presenting your company the Google of X, the Facebook of Y or the Kayak of Z to investors can help VCs quickly get a sense for your business plan, it encourages investors to focus on why the comparison is not appropriate. As a result, it seems that every time an entrepreneur makes an explicit comparison between his company and an existing category leader, investors retort with "except your company [doesn't have the same barriers, has smaller margins, has a longer sales cycle, has a smaller addressable market, has more competitors, or has stronger gatekeepers.]" Almost without fail, this sales-y one-line explanation of your company drives investors to focus on relative inferiorities of your business.

I think you're almost always better off staying away from these comparisons. Instead of describing your company as being similar to an existing player in another market, just focus on explaining the nuts and bolts of what your company does. If an investor draws that same comparison, that's great, but otherwise (as they say), don't lead with your chin.

MAKE YOUR PRESENTATION FUN

At minimum, presentations need to address all key topics an investor needs to learn about your business. Just because these topics are considered dry (by anyone who is not a tech business nerd, such as myself) doesn't mean that you can't make the presentation more fun for investors to hear.

I have seen a variety of approaches to fun presentations over time. Some use characters or cartoons to tell stories and others use gripping pictures to bring concepts to life. If you can integrate fun elements into your presentations (without being too childish) you may be better off for a few reasons.

First, fun presentations set the tone of the meeting. A playful presentation is more likely to facilitate a more lighthearted conversation with the investors. While this doesn't mean that tough questions won't be asked, it can transform cold poker faces into light-hearted laughing counterparties.

Second, these presentations can be more memorable. Being memorable is not only important for keeping your business top of mind with overloaded investors, but it can also help them remember key nuances of your business that will help them make the case to their partners.

Investors hear a lot of business ideas each week. If you keep the humor professional and mature, having a little fun with the presentation might help you stand out and get to the next step in the process.

The How

THE OPERATIONAL FINANCIAL MODEL

While most entrepreneurs have completed a business plan and PowerPoint presentation prior to a first meeting, not all have finalized a financial model, let alone made a financial model that is "operational." An operational financial model does more than show projections; it explains "how" you are going to build the business. It does this by not only highlighting the outputs (e.g., projected revenue, EBITDA, headcount, etc.), but also by clearly demonstrating the inputs and their relationship to the business.

Put another way, the most detailed calculations and assumptions of the model should be transparent. This clarity is absolutely critical for helping VCs understand both your projections and your business. Unfortunately, most entrepreneurs submit incomplete models to VCs, assuming that only the outputs are important, leaving the VC to invest time in unraveling the mess of inputs and calculations.

If you take the time to clearly format and label the inputs that drive your model, VCs will be able to gut-check the reasonableness of your assumptions. If they believe the assumptions, they will be more comfortable with the output of the model.

Detailing your assumptions will also help VCs understand your business model. These inputs will demonstrate your view of what drives revenue and profitability, helping VCs to understand your logic and evaluate how your strategic plan is connected to driving financial growth.

Lastly, if the calculations in your model are easy to follow, VCs will be able both to understand how you think about your business and assess your logic. The best way to make the calculations easy to follow is by carefully formatting and labeling each cell and by limiting each cell to only basic calculations. Spread long equations out into several small calculations. While constructing the model in this way will require more spreadsheet cells to get through the math, it will be far easier to audit.

Remember that although VCs are interested in more than the output of the model, they also want to understand the "how." Your model can help to answer those questions. Ultimately, creating a transparent model can help VCs understand and get excited about your company and your ability to manage it.

EVOLVE YOUR FINANCIAL MODEL

After VCs have evaluated your financial model, they may ask you to consider some additional scenarios. They may ask if there are scenarios whereby your company can extend its runway on a fixed amount of capital, increase revenues with more capital or operate with less capital under management.

Investors typically ask these questions for three reasons:

1. To understand the drivers of the business,
2. To identify investment structures that are a fit with their investment strategies, and
3. To ensure your company takes an investment that will be helpful to the business.

By understanding the drivers of the business, investors can help management teams ensure that they are operating the business to perform optimally. For example, if reducing the company's burn doesn't substantially impact its ability to generate revenue, there may be too much "fat" in the company's spend – an issue worth evaluating.

VCs also need to make investments that are consistent with their investment theses, while ensuring that the company has enough runway to achieve milestones and be positioned for its subsequent capital raise. Furthermore, VCs may ask you to evolve your capital requirements to align the investment opportunity with their investment strategy.

You should try to accommodate these types of financial model reviews. Here are three reasons:

1. They will help investors better understand your business,
2. They position you to develop a productive working relationship with future board members, and
3. They help ensure that you are deploying capital most effectively.

It's worth noting that in order to engage in these types of scenario discussions you must ensure that your financial model is driven by variables that enable the creation of scenarios.

VCS DO NOT WANT YOUR COMPANY TO BE PROFITABLE (IN THE SHORT TERM)

VCs are not focused on the short-term profitability of your company. This might seem counter-intuitive at first since turning a profit is the objective of most businesses. However, rather than focusing on maximizing profits, VCs are focused on maximizing shareholder value. When shareholder value is maximized the value of the company at exit is maximized – that's the big win for everyone: VCs and entrepreneurs.

Most VCs invest in high growth companies where would-be profits can be re-invested to stimulate growth. Growth in these companies creates more shareholder value than profits paid out as dividends. As a result, VCs generally encourage management to invest all or most excess cash in growth opportunities until the high value opportunities are exhausted. When these opportunities are exhausted less cash will be reinvested, yielding a healthy profit.

When you are speaking with VCs and walking them through your model, understand that they will be more focused on revenue growth in the short term. However, in the medium-term, they will want to understand how profitable the company can be.

THE PRE-FUNDRAISING PROCESS

Get Tactical Before You Get Started

HOW TO GAUGE VC INTEREST IN YOUR COMPANY EARLY

The fundraising process is different for each startup. Some entrepreneurs have a swarm of VCs chasing them immediately, some find one or two interested investors after a long process and others never find a suitor. The challenge is that it's very hard for most entrepreneurs to know which scenario to expect when they start raising money. As a result, there seems to be a lot of confusion about when to start raising money.

The best way to prepare for this process is to take the temperature of the market early. You should try to connect with VCs long before you plan to raise money. When you meet them, tell them you are not yet raising money, but would be interested to get their feedback on your idea. Asking the question this way affords you the opportunity to learn more about the likely interest in your company in a way that could create interest in itself.

Positioning the question this way should create a favorable dynamic with the VC. VCs love to be the first one to know about startups, as it means that they may be able to make an investment before other investors learn about the opportunity. This early feedback tactic should create more interest with the VC; the opportunity becomes sexier. You give them this access and in return you get to hear an early reaction.

In addition to the appeal of learning about your company early, every VC (like everyone else) wants what they can't have. By engaging them early when you are not ready to accept their money, you will be sending a message that you have something that they can't have ... yet. This should also increase the appeal of your company.

WHAT TO DO IF THE VC AGREES TO GIVE YOU FEEDBACK

If the VC bites after you place the bait, be prepared to engage in a process akin to the traditional review process. This means the first step will typically still be your submitting an executive summary. Therefore, you should have your executive summary ready before you start the process.

Barring special situations and relationships you will not likely skip right to the initial call or meeting step in the process. VCs are busy and prefer executive summary reviews because they are more time efficient, even if you have successfully piqued their interest.

HOW TO INTERPRET VC RESPONSE TO YOUR MARKET TESTING

Meeting with VCs early will enable you to get a sense for one investor's interest level well before you go out to market to raise money, enabling you to better predict how much time to allot to the process.

- If the VC expresses interest in learning more and potentially investing now, you'll know that it might not take long to raise money in the future.
- If they point out some concerns but suggest that you stay in touch, you might be in more a medium to long process and you'll need to start early.
- And, if they give you feedback but no indication of interest, you might fall into either of the long fundraising process or will never raise capital categories.

It's worth taking this feedback with a grain of salt; VCs have very different views of the world and it's possible that the VCs you spoke with may not be the best indication of the market for your company. If they didn't indicate any interest, the best way to interpret the implications of their feedback for your company's fundraising future is to determine what type of feedback they gave you.

Here are three reasons why a VC might not be interested and their implications for you:

1. If it's a business model concern, you may want to re-evaluate your business.
2. If it's an investment opportunity issue you should re-evaluate your fundraising strategy; VCs may not be the right fit.
3. If it was a fit with the thesis issue, you may simply need to find the right VC.

HOW TESTING THE VC MARKET CAN LEAD TO AN INVESTMENT: BEING MONITORED

If the VC gets interested early, you may be able to convert this market testing exercise into an investment. If you find that the VC gets excited about what you are doing, they may take one of three courses of action: monitor your progress, conduct due diligence or put down a term sheet.

If they are interested but feel that some milestones need to be achieved before they can invest, they may want to monitor your progress. This is a great outcome. It is an opportunity for the entrepreneur to push the company forward knowing that there is a light of potential interest at the end of the tunnel.

If you find yourself in this situation, you will have three objectives.

1. To continue driving the company forward
2. To continue to create momentum with your interested VC
3. To engage other investors in tandem when the timing is right for your company

HOW TESTING THE VC MARKET CAN LEAD TO AN INVESTMENT: BEGINNING DUE DILIGENCE

Another outcome of early VC interest is due diligence. If the VC begins conducting due diligence and you are interested in taking their money, you will need to gear up for the process that I describe in my chapter on due diligence.

This can be a daunting challenge for entrepreneurs who are very early in the process of building their companies. However, good VCs will understand the additional constraints associated with these stages of a startup and adjust expectations accordingly. They will know that you won't have customers to call, your model won't be fully baked and your marketing plan will still be buried in the back of your mind.

HOW TESTING THE VC MARKET CAN LEAD TO AN INVESTMENT: GOING STRAIGHT TO TERM SHEET

A third outcome of early VC interest in the testing stage is going straight to term sheet. In rare cases VCs will ask you in to meet their partners, conduct an accelerated due diligence process and offer you a term sheet. If this happens you can be sure that the investor is pretty excited about your company.

In this scenario, it's likely that you will have other VCs interested in your company in the future. However, in my opinion the wise entrepreneurs will try to do the right deal with this VC. There are a few reasons for this:

1. If you get the right deal done early you can focus on building your company, avoiding the painful and distracting process of raising capital.

2. A lot can go wrong with your company over time that could prevent you from being funded in the future. Microsoft or Google might launch a similar product, your partner might quit or you might not land that partnership that you were so close to getting when the VC laid down the term sheet.

3. The venture market or broader economy might take a turn for the worse, changing funding dynamics and making it hard to raise capital in the future.

4. If the investor is this excited about your company they share your vision and are more likely to be highly motivated to help you in the ways that they should.

THE BEST TIME TO RAISE MONEY IS WHEN YOU CAN

It is not uncommon for entrepreneurs to tell VCs that they are not yet raising capital. There is nothing wrong with taking this approach, as it can enable founders to engage in pre-fundraising activities such as demonstrating a trend or gauging VC interest, before they begin fundraising.

It is important to be ready to engage VCs when they get interested in your company, even if you are not officially fundraising. VCs can become interested in your company before you plan to raise money.

In some cases, entrepreneurs can be caught off guard by preemptive VC interest, leading them to slow down the process or disengage until they are officially ready to raise money. Some entrepreneurs have a plan and want to follow it religiously. Unfortunately, this strategy can lead to missed opportunities.

The best time to raise money is when you can. The wisdom in this statement comes from the fact that early-stage decision making is often more art than science; market changes, economic shifts or other more exciting opportunities can lead a VC to lose interest in the deal they were most excited about last week.

To be clear, this doesn't mean that you should take money that you don't need – too much capital can make your company inefficient. The point here is that it is worthwhile to be flexible with the timing of your fundraising – if you have the opportunity to take capital six months earlier than expected, you probably should do it.

Walking away from an interested investor because of the timing can be a dangerous move. At the very least, it may mean one fewer investor to drive up the price of your company. At the very most, it may mean your company misses the opportunity to raise capital altogether.

GETTING THE MEETING

The Approach

THE ELEVATOR PITCH IS DEAD

When I first started attending panels and VC events, there was a lot of hype around the concept of an elevator pitch. An elevator pitch is an overview of a new business idea that an entrepreneur can explain to an investor in the length of a chance elevator ride shared by the two parties. In approximately one minute, the entrepreneur needs to bait and hook a VC in order to reel the investor in later.

At business plan competitions and pitch events, pitch coaches spent hours with entrepreneurs sharing with them the secrets of the arcane art of the elevator pitch. And once their disciples were fully indoctrinated, the newbies would get to show off their elevator pitching skills. Most entrepreneurs are trained to pack as much information as possible into that minute, driving most pitches to sound like they were being delivered by the spokesman for MicroMachines.

While there are always cases where stories hyped by the media and entrepreneur folklore do come to life (I suppose entrepreneurs do on occasion share elevators with VCs), this generally isn't how business gets done. While entrepreneurs can meet investors at networking events, at pitch events and, yes, in elevators, they don't need to feel that they have to corner the investor and deliver a canned one-minute light-speed monologue about their business before the investor can get away.

More commonly, when an investor meets an entrepreneur, the former wants to know what the latter is working on and will typically ask. Investors by nature are seeking great entrepreneurs and are therefore likely to be interested in hearing the pitch if they think they are speaking to a credible person. Because the investor is interested in hearing a little bit about the business if it matches their interests (sector and otherwise), entrepreneurs will typically get to describe their business through the course of a regular conversation, not a monologue. You don't have to trap them and you don't have to rush.

When asked what they're working on, good entrepreneurs provide a plain English overview of the company (and sometimes describe the pain point when it's not obvious). That explanation can come in as little as one sentence – "We're helping people do X by offering a service that does Y." Typically, if an investor doesn't get it from your description, they'll ask some clarifying questions. And, if they're interested in learning more about key elements of the opportunity (market, competition, etc.) an investor will ask.

In some cases, investors will ask the entrepreneur to send along an executive summary after just hearing the overview of the service or after a few questions. The executive summary is the document that should fill in the rest of the blanks about the business – as explained in my earlier chapter on materials, this document should cover all of the other elements that are often packed into an elevator pitch.

In other situations, the investor will determine that the opportunity isn't a fit for them and not ask for any more information. That's an okay outcome for entrepreneurs, too – they don't have to waste time with an investor who isn't going to get interested.

While I do think you should be able to speak succinctly and intelligently about your business, I don't think you need to have a canned elevator pitch on hand. Ultimately, I contend that elevator pitches are relevant for pitch events and not much else.

WHY VCS MAY CALL

Venture capital funds find investments in different ways. Some passively receive executive summaries from their personal networks and do very little searching. Others actively scour the marketplace for interesting companies.

Those who actively scour the marketplace may contact you directly without warning and without an introduction. The initial contact may be made via email or phone – that's determined by the individual style of the VC.

Typically, this initial contact will come after your company has received some publicity, bringing you to the attention of the investor community. The most common types of publicity that attract VC attention are press or presence at tradeshows. As a result, when your company comes out of stealth mode, you should be prepared for inbound VC contact (stealth mode is a temporary phase of secretiveness, usually to avoid alerting competitors to a pending product launch).

When you are contacted by a VC, you need to be prepared to explain your business touching on the key topics, answer questions succinctly and send an executive summary.

You unofficially begin your fundraising process when you enter the public consciousness. When you are preparing to come out of stealth mode, you should know whether or not you want to raise venture capital and you should be prepared to engage investors.

WHY AN EXECUTIVE SUMMARY

Your first submission to a VC should be an executive summary, not a complete business plan. A complete business plan attempts to tell a VC everything there is to know about your company. At this stage in the process there are too many other plans being submitted; VCs do not have time to learn everything about every company.

In this early part of the review process, VCs are not trying to decide whether or not they will invest in a company; VCs are just trying to figure out if there is a possibility that they will invest, given the high-level characteristics of the business. Since there are a lot of these submissions to review, they need to quickly decide if they want to learn more or pass.

As a result, entrepreneurs should aim to work within this process by submitting a clear and concise executive summary (as described previously in the Preparing Your Materials chapter). The purpose of an executive summary is to get the first meeting. Don't try to rush the process. Focus constantly on getting to the next level.

SUBMITTING YOUR EXECUTIVE SUMMARY

The first step in the meeting process is submitting your executive summary. There are lots of ways to submit your executive summary: cold channels (e.g., cold email or cold LinkedIn introduction), through introducing yourself to a

VC at a networking event or through a third party introduction (e.g., a lawyer or mutual contact). While the VC is likely to read your executive summary and respond in any scenario, the plan can be at a disadvantage if it comes from a less familiar source.

When a VC receives an executive summary from a trusted source (e.g., someone who has sent good deals to them before), they expect the idea to have gone through another filter before it was sent to them; they expect the idea to be better. These will therefore receive more attention.

With this in mind, savvy entrepreneurs generally try to have their business plans submitted through a mutual contact. Knowing that savvy entrepreneurs understand this bias makes VCs even more predisposed to favor submissions from familiar sources, since the entrepreneurs who are also good at networking (which is a determinant of success for companies that require partners or business customers) will find a way to network their way to a VC. Finding a way to submit through a mutual contact has become the VC's first way of assessing management.

Submitting your plan is the first step in the fundraising process and therefore it is also your first impression. It's important to understand that VCs appreciate an entrepreneur's ability to create a warm introduction – you should try to do this if you can. However, if you really don't have a viable way for making that happen, don't hesitate to get your business plan in through a cold channel. A first impression does not trump a good idea.

GET THE VC'S ATTENTION: USE THE RIGHT SUBJECT

When emailing an investor, you should think of every word in the email as an opportunity to get your message across. One part of the email that is typically underutilized is the subject line. Great subject lines can pique the interest of not only the first recipient of your email, but also anyone else to whom the email is forwarded.

Despite this, most emails are given generic subjects like "investment opportunity," "introduction" or "startup." This is a missed opportunity.

The best way to make your subject line memorable, relevant and catchy is to use your company's mission statement, as it should be concise while making clear the pain point that you intend to solve. However, you should also be sure that your mission statement is associated with your company's name. The best subjects follow this format: "Name: Mission statement." For example, "Google: Making the world's information accessible."

It's important to be concise, because depending on the view setting of the investor's inbox, part of the subject may be cut off.

FIRST CONTACT: DO NOT SPAM THE WHOLE PARTNERSHIP

Another mistake that entrepreneurs make is submitting their business plan to the entire partnership of one fund (unless you happen to know all of the partners at that fund). Doing so is considered rather impersonal and calls into question your business judgment.

If it isn't obvious, here are some reasons why this is a bad idea:

First and foremost, doing a mass email raises red flags to the VC about your competency. Part of being competent means understanding the nuances of business interactions. VCs prefer entrepreneurs who can leverage their relationships to get introduced to a VC or who have the wherewithal to create a connection with the VC during the initial touch point. Doing neither makes VCs think you don't understand how to operate effectively.

Second, not only does this action reflect a lack of judgment, it reflects a lack of concern. Entrepreneurs should seek to understand who we are as a firm and as individuals – the form letter makes it appear as though we were simply part of a mailing list. Not all VCs are created equal and not all VCs are going to be a fit for this entrepreneur. If an entrepreneur is not thoughtful about his fundraising, why should anyone believe that he'll be thoughtful about other aspects of his business in the future?

Third, this is a missed opportunity. An entrepreneur missed the opportunity to create a connection with one of the partners during that initial email.

Ultimately, spamming a partnership with your executive summary is a bad idea. Try to find firms that would complement your venture and leverage your relationships to connect with them in a more constructive manner.

HOW NOT TO SUBMIT AN EXECUTIVE SUMMARY

On occasion, entrepreneurs mass-email dozens, or even hundreds, of VCs their executive summaries. To make matters worse, in some cases the entrepreneurs carbon copy all of the venture capitalists, enabling all of them to see what the person had done. In other situations, they use a mail merge to mass-email VCs, which is also often transparent a transparent tactic to VCs.

Needless to say, these are approaches are a bad idea. This strategy decreases the likelihood that the individual would be funded. What these approaches most often accomplish is ensuring that there are hundreds of VCs who don't want to hear about this business idea since they know the entrepreneur is not a competent manager.

This approach not only indicates a degree of laziness, but also highlights a lack of understanding around the human side of business. If an entrepreneur doesn't understand the nuance of the fundraising process, a VC might assume that they don't have the chops to understand the art of selling their product.

Do yourself a favor and be thoughtful about how you submit your business plan.

TO WHOM SHOULD YOU SUBMIT YOUR EXECUTIVE SUMMARY?

Selecting the right partner at a venture fund to submit your executive summary to can significantly increase your odds of being asked in for a meeting. In cases where you don't have an existing relationship or a mutual contact with any of the partners, the key is to find someone who shares common interests with you. Common interests can be related to your business or to your personal life.

First, identify the partner who would identify with your business. There is usually some degree of specialization within a venture fund – each partner focuses on sectors that reflect their career experience before becoming a VC and from the boards they sit on as a VC. If there is a partner who focuses on your sector or industry, you should try to get your executive summary to that person; their expertise is likely to help to more rapidly understand your vision, increasing the odds that they will want to learn more.

Whether you find a partner at the fund with sector expertise or not, you should try to find common ground on a personal level to warm up the relationship. In your introductory email, your first direct email to the partner, you should let the partner know what you have in common. This could include: growing up in the same town, having studied at the same place, belonging to the same country club, having a mutual friend, going to the same industry conferences or sharing the same hobbies (e.g., a sport).

While information about the partner's background and interests may not be readily available, you should be able to find a good bit of info by scouring certain websites, such as LinkedIn.

In some instances, the partner who focuses on your sector may not be the person with whom you have common interests. In this case, you should copy both people on one email that introduces the company and highlights the common ground that you have with one of the partners. If you send separate emails, the person who has common ground with you may forget to tell the sector specialist that you are more interesting than average – information that could significantly increase your traction with the sector expert (who is likely to take his partner's favoritism into account).

It's a surprisingly small world. Even if you don't have an existing relationship or mutual contact with any of the partners, there are good odds that you have something in common with at least on partner at each firm. Take the time to find your common ground – it will pave the path of least resistance.

HOW TO DRAW ATTENTION TO YOUR EXECUTIVE SUMMARY

The best VCs receive dozens of business plans each week, often creating a daunting pile of executive summaries for the VC to evaluate. In order to keep up, VCs need to review each of these plans relatively quickly, often allocating just a few minutes to each executive summary. The fact that these reviews are done quickly isn't a secret – many entrepreneurs know this, and some of the more aggressive founders employ tactics to draw more attention to their business plan. Some have tried to make their email catchy by referencing other VCs with whom they are speaking or linking to recent press coverage that they have received. Others have mailed a follow-on hard copy of the plan, a sample product or even a book related to the topic.

These tactics are driven by two objectives. The first is to make sure the business plan is reviewed, and the second is to get the investor interested enough to want to learn more. These attention-grabbing tactics might get your plan reviewed, but far and away the most effective tactic for getting your materials reviewed is to send them to a VC who has a reputation for being responsive. Getting the plan into the right hands from the beginning will do more for your odds than any tactics you deploy.

The best way to achieve the second objective, getting the investor to want to learn more, is to have a professional appearing and complete executive summary, submitted through a trusted channel. Since sophisticated investors are focused on identifying investment opportunities that are within their investment thesis, their level of interest is essentially a function of the quality of the opportunity (the idea, the team, the market, etc).

In addition to not being helpful in generating interest, with few exceptions, the attention-grabbing tactics mentioned above can actually be harmful.

First, giving investors books or hard copies of the business plan does little to influence decision-making. While the investors may appreciate the book, it's unlikely that they'll have time to read it before making a decision about your business plan. Furthermore, while submitting hard copies can draw more attention, it also might imply to some that you are less tech-savvy, a potential challenge for tech entrepreneurs.

Additionally, citing other investors with whom you are speaking is a risky tactic, as it can create problems for you. While this ploy is designed to give you credibility, it can have the opposite effect. If the targeted investor contacts one of the cited VCs and hears that the cited VC does not like the idea or has already passed on the opportunity to invest, your odds of being further engaged may be limited.

On the other hand, citing recent press can be effective as it both demonstrates that your organization is able to attract the attention of news publications and enables the VC to learn more about your business plan through the press coverage.

In sum, do your research before submitting your executive summary. Getting your plan into the hands of a responsive investor who focuses on your type of business is the most effective way to get traction. After you have done that, however, be selective in leveraging tactics. Make sure that you only use tactics that will help you achieve your objectives.

DON'T SEND VCS PAINFULLY LONG EMAILS

Mark Twain once said, "If I had more time I would write a shorter letter."

As this quote suggests, it is often more difficult to be concise. Getting to the point, however, is important when you're communicating with a VC as sending long emails may make getting an investor to "yes" more challenging. There are two key reasons why sending long emails (more than two paragraphs) can hurt you.

First, since VCs are relatively busy folks, when they see a long email, it's often slightly irritating. They're frustrated to spend a lot of time reading a long email to understand what could be delivered in just a few sentences. Furthermore, your interactions early in the fundraising process signal to the VC what it will be like to interact with you over the duration of the venture, meaning these VCs expect that investing in you may mean years of not-to-the-point communication.

Second, in an effort to save time, many time-crunched investors have learned to skim long emails, searching for just the key messages. Skimming is an art, not a science, and your key points may be missed. If sentence number 34 of your monologue is intended to be your drive-it-home message, investors may never read the words that you thought were most important.

While writing long emails is only a minor crime, it's one worth avoiding. Doing so will make you more effective in the fundraising process.

DOMAIN DISCRIMINATION

Domain discrimination is the act by which tech snobs judge people based upon email domain. When I first heard of this concept I thought it was a joke, but I now believe that this is a fairly prevalent (albeit minor) form of discrimination in the tech community.

To be clear, while there are numerous considerations for creating a professional email address, I am referring solely to which email service provider you choose to use (e.g., Yahoo!, Gmail, AOL, Hotmail or other). I believe that this is one basis by which members of the tech community form first impressions.

Ultimately, I suspect that this judgment comes from the view that your email domain puts a time stamp on the extent to which you are current with the latest technologies. Many would argue that email service providers have not evolved substantially from their initial offerings, but they have become increasingly dated and represent somewhat clear generations in the evolution of email technology. The logic follows as such: If you're using an older platform, you're likely using a service with less functionality and therefore are seen by bleeding edge technology adopters to be behind, outdated and not as technologically savvy.

It is worth noting, however, that email addresses using company or private domains appear to be well-respected. The judgment appears to be limited to the decision to use a less technologically advanced service over a more advanced once – especially when they're both free.

I recognize that for many, the choice to stay on one email platform is merely an attempt to avoid the pain of informing all of your contacts about your new email address. I believe, however, that the perception remains.

I don't have a good solution for changing this mechanism for forming opinions, but I do think it's worthwhile to understand. While in the venture capital decision-making process this topic receives very little consideration, I suspect that it does inevitably play a very small role in the all-important first impression you make on many technology-focused VCs. When you submit an executive summary from a very outdated email platform, some of these VCs take notice, consciously or not. As such, you may want to signal your tech savvy by using one of the more modern email platforms. Doing so may or may not help you make a good first impression, but it can't hurt.

AVOID DEMANDING THE LAST MINUTE MEETING

It's not uncommon for entrepreneurs to want to meet with VCs in a destination geography when they're in town for business meetings or conferences. It makes sense to get more out of a business trip. While this is generally a smart strategy, trying to schedule your VC meetings at the last minute will likely lead to missed opportunities.

It's important to understand that sending an investor an email stating that your team will be in town in a few days and would like to meet is not a practical strategy. There are two key reasons for this. First, VCs generally keep a busy schedule and might be booked a few weeks out. Second, VCs will often want to screen your business plan or have an initial phone conversation prior to agreeing to meet with your team. This additional step in the process may add days or even weeks to the process depending on how busy they are.

Inevitably there are times when the business trip is planned at the last minute. There may be little that you can do to contact investors early. If you do know you are going to be making a business trip and want to meet with investors, however, engage them as soon as possible.

BE NICE TO ASSISTANTS

Some entrepreneurs are rude to executive assistants, treating them as second-class members of a VC team. While assistants aren't directly involved in the investment decision-making process, they do have important influence.

Most VC firms have few employees. As in any small group, there is "water cooler" talk, ensuring that most people know the dirt on lots of topics. Assistants participate in this process.

When an entrepreneur is rude to an assistant, the professional staff will definitely hear about it. Since the professional staff seeks to back people with good judgment, this can count as a strike against the entrepreneur.

If you don't broadly treat people with respect in life (which is preferred), at least be strategic enough to know that every impression you make on someone affiliated with a VC fund will impact the probability of your receiving an investment.

What to Expect

VCS ARE UNAVAILABLE ON MONDAY

For most VC funds, Monday is a quasi-holy day. Most VCs do not schedule meetings or calls on Mondays in order to have a partners meeting where the team can have uninterrupted time to discuss deals and generally manage the business. They do this because the other four days of the work week are typically full of entrepreneur meetings, due diligence calls, investor follow-ups, networking events and administrative work, leaving little to no time for the partners to meet and make decisions.

There are a few takeaways from this for entrepreneurs:

- If you need to have a call, lunch or meeting with a VC, don't expect it to happen on Monday.
- You shouldn't get frustrated if a VC doesn't respond to your email on a Monday, as they may not get to first look at their email until Tuesday.
- If you want a partnership to make a decision about your business, try to get them all of the requisite information before the next Monday meeting. If you wait until a Tuesday to send them the information that they requested, they may not be able to discuss your venture until the following Monday; you could lose a week and some momentum along with it.
- Showing that you are aware that most VCs have their partners' meetings on Mondays also demonstrates that you understand how a VC operates.

If you are aware of the fact that VCs typically have a partner's meeting on Monday, you will be better able to manage the pace of communication.

WHY A VC MAY BE SLOW TO RESPOND

After submitting your executive summary, you may not receive a response for several weeks. While this can be frustrating, do not let it discourage you.

Generally, venture capital funds are small practices; there are only a few investment professionals. With so few people on the team, everyone is required to play numerous roles, from managing the company to making investments. The old drinking from a fire hose image applies here. To put a finer point on this, VCs juggle:

- Raising money,
- Providing their investors with ongoing support (e.g., reporting),
- Managing the office (vendors, support staff, administrative processes),
- Working with lawyers and accountants to make sure everything is done properly,
- Attending frequent board meetings to support their portfolio companies,
- Marketing their fund by attending industry events and conferences,
- Reviewing thousands of business plans,
- Meeting with entrepreneurs, and
- Finding time to have a life.

If anyone should understand the pace of this job, it's entrepreneurs who also juggle all of the facets of a company.

My reason for spelling this out is not to generate sympathy for VCs; it's to help entrepreneurs understand why a VCs may seem unresponsive at times. Expect VCs to be perpetually behind; there are always piles of tasks that they still have to get to. Reviewing your executive summary may be in one of those piles. Therefore, if you haven't heard back from a VC regarding your executive summary, do not get discouraged (even if it has been several weeks).

If it has been a while since you submitted your executive summary, it's appropriate to politely follow up with a VC. In most cases, VCs will know that they owe you a response. A little nudging may compel them to review your plan and take the next step.

WHY VCS DO NOT SIGN NDAS

First-time entrepreneurs sometimes ask VCs to sign NDAs (non-disclosure agreements). They do this because they are worried that their intellectual property will not be protected without a legal agreement in place.

To the surprise of these individuals, most VCs do not sign NDAs. However, in my opinion that doesn't mean that the entrepreneur is entirely unprotected.

While there are always exceptions, most VCs follow an informal code of ethics when it comes to intellectual property. Most VCs follow this code for a few reasons. First, they protect people's intellectual property because it's the right thing to do. Second, they have a market-driven incentive to protect intellectual property, as a failure to do so would create a professional risk. A reputation of betraying this code would dissuade entrepreneurs from bringing opportunities to them, preventing them from being good at their job.

In addition to these reasons, VCs can't afford to invest the time or money in having lawyers evaluate NDAs for every company that the review. VCs typically review thousands of business plans a year – if they had to pay lawyers to evaluate thousands of NDAs and spend time reading thousands of NDAs, they wouldn't get much else done. Ultimately this would create prohibitive cost and time requirements.

Furthermore, there are frequently numerous startups trying to solve the same problem. VCs may meet with many of them and it takes VCs a while to figure out which company they want to back. If they had to sign NDAs with each company before hearing their pitch, there would inevitably be companies taking action against them when they join the board of one of the players (even though they still follow the code of ethics).

Based on that, it's generally not a good idea to ask a VC to sign an NDA, as it will make you look naive. If you are not comfortable with discussing your business with VCs without a legal document in place, then it may make sense for you to look for angel investors who will sign an NDA.

In my opinion, the best way to protect yourself is to make sure that you are pitching to VCs who are not on the board of a competitive company. Beyond that, VCs are generally ethical professionals and are, in my opinion, a safe group to speak with.

BEING INVITED FOR A CALL

If your executive summary gets a VC interested, they will typically invite you in for a meeting or a call.

While the process varies by VC fund, a call typically means one of two things. Either the VC is interested in having you in for a meeting, but can't because of circumstantial issues (e.g., scheduling), or the VC needs a few high-level questions answered in order to see if you fit the investment criteria and determine if he wants to invite you in for a meeting.

All of the key high-level questions should be answered by a well-prepared executive summary, so being asked for a call should compel you to revisit your materials.

Try to figure out why you are being asked for a call as soon as possible, as it will help you figure out what you need to accomplish on the call. If you were asked for a call because the VC didn't have time to meet, your objective should be to "win" a meeting by sharing the next layer of the plan as they ask questions. If you're on the call because the executive summary didn't answer all of their high-level questions, your objective should be to fill in the blanks. Don't provide them with tons of extraneous information; just give them what they need so that they can decide whether they want to invite you in for a meeting. Usually, their decision to have a meeting with you hinges on the one or two questions they had in mind before the call. Answer those clearly and concisely and then ask for a meeting.

Don't forget that the call is your first impression. While the VC only asked for the call to have a few questions answered, they will be assessing your compatibility and competency. Be prepared to put your best foot forward.

Why You Might Get Dinged

WHY YOU MIGHT NOT GET THE MEETING

Not being invited to have a meeting with a venture fund does not mean that

VCs think your idea is bad.

As I have stated above, VCs are very busy. They try to save time by only meeting with companies they think they may invest in. In order to invest in a company, the idea needs to meet three criteria – being a good business idea is not enough. In order to invest, your company must be:

1. A viable, high growth, scalable business,
2. A good investment, capable of a large return, and
3. Aligned with the fund's investment criteria.

To reiterate this point, you may have a great business idea and VCs may expect you to do very well for yourself, but that does not mean they want to invest. In order for you to be a good investment, the current valuation needs to be reasonable and the company needs to have both the potential and the entrepreneur's desire to grow to target levels. In order for a good investment to be a fit for a fund, the company has to play in the right sector and have other specific properties that align with the VC's pre-determined criteria.

Investment strategies vary significantly by fund. What interests one VC may not be desirable to another. As a result, entrepreneurs should not interpret a lack of interest as a judgment of their idea. Your company may simply not meet the pre-determined criteria for that fund.

Usually you can find a fund's investment criteria on their website.

Understanding this dynamic can save you a lot of time when you are fundraising. Target numerous funds that invest in companies like yours and expect some not to be interested even if your idea is exceptional.

VCS HAVE FLASHBACK SYNDROME

Another less common cause is the fact that VCs get flashbacks.

Experienced VCs have invested in lots of companies and inevitably some of those companies failed. When a VC sees a new company that is similar to a failed previous investment, VCs tend to shy away. I'm not certain that this behavior is entirely rational or objective, as some investments fail simply because they were too early to market, they had the wrong management or because they were just unlucky. Nonetheless, a VC's scar tissue does impact their investment decision making and can therefore affect your fundraising prospects.

The good news is that few VCs have made exactly the same types of investments. It is not likely you will encounter more than one rejection from a flashback.

ANOTHER REASON YOU MAY BE REJECTED: PORTFOLIO CONCENTRATION

VCs try to increase the odds of their portfolio returns being high by diversifying their investments across industry sectors. This way, if one sector tanks, the portfolio could still generate an attractive return. As a result, if a VC already has significant exposure to the market in which you operate, they may be less inclined to invest.

However, portfolio concentration is not typically the key consideration in making an investment decision. If an outstanding company is presented to them, they may be willing to assume the additional exposure to a sector. Therefore, portfolio concentration becomes increasingly significant if your company only generates average interest amongst the partners.

SIGNS THAT YOUR TEAM MIGHT BE DETERRING INVESTORS

VCs pass on investment opportunities for a whole host of reasons having to do with the business, personal experiences or the makeup of the existing portfolio. But the reason VCs are least likely to cite is one of the most common reasons for deciding not to invest: entrepreneur competency.

It's important for entrepreneurs to consistently try to demonstrate competency in the fundraising process. This is critical because the team is a key part of the investment decision; VCs are investing in more than an idea, they are investing in the individuals who will run the startup.

VCs, however, have a tough time telling entrepreneurs that team is the reason that they are not going to invest. I think this is understandable – telling a founder that you like the idea but won't invest in them is usually taken as an offensive statement. Furthermore, in an environment where an investor's reputation is a critical driver of his success, offending entrepreneurs can be a career-hindering move that VCs would prefer to avoid.

This begs that question: if VCs often decide not to invest in a company because of the team, but won't tell the entrepreneurs, how can entrepreneurs figure out that they're scaring away the VCs? There are a couple of ways.

First, if you find that your team has great success in obtaining lots of meetings with investors based upon the merit of the idea but find that investors quickly pass after meeting you and your partners, the team may be the problem.

Second, if investors seem to spend a decent bit of time delicately probing about the team, asking questions like, "What gaps exist in your team as it stands today?" or, "What are your current roles, and how do you see those evolving over time?" investors may have concerns about your company's leadership.

If you are comfortable bringing in new leadership, you can proactively state that you are willing to do so if the collective opinion is that this would be the best move for the company. If investors are interested in making a change in the company's leadership, this prompt could give them the opportunity to explore that with you without being offensive. Alternatively, if they communicate that they don't think a change would be necessary in the short term, you'll know you don't have a team issue.

THE UNSAID REASON VCS MAY NOT BACK YOU: RESOURCE EFFICIENCY

When VCs are asked what their investment criteria are, they will list off a number of common considerations: big market size, competitive advantage, a specific geography, a target stage, etc. There is, however, another important consideration not often mentioned: the resource efficiency of the company.

Resource efficiency refers to how much value can be created through the company with a given amount of resources.

Note that this definition refers to value, not revenue. While revenue is often a driver of value, there are other types of value: technology assets, customers, etc. YouTube is a prime example of a company that created substantial value without generating revenue.

Also note that the definition refers to resources, not capital. While the most measurable resource on the market is capital; time, knowledge and other resources are also important considerations. Many of the tech-light companies on the market today are less capital intensive, but that doesn't mean that the companies don't consume substantial resources. The most typical resource consumed is time on the part of management and investors.

Using this framework, there are broadly two types of categories that companies fall into: linear or exponential growers. Linear growers increase the value of the company in proportion to the amount of resources invested in the company. Exponential growers realize increased efficiencies over time – for every additional unit of resource invested in the company the value increases more than it did for the prior unit of resource. Simply put, in an exponential growth company the next million dollars of investment or unit of time creates more value than the prior million dollars or unit of time.

In general, linear growth companies sell a tangible good or a labor-dependent service where one more employee generates a proportional increase in revenue. Consumer products, consulting, investment banking, services, recruiting and others are obvious types of linear growth companies. It is worth noting, however, that while these linear growth businesses do realize increased efficiency over time, especially as back-office functions are scaled, the effects of their scale is less robust than in other companies.

Exponential growth companies often have a single asset that can be leveraged across an increasing number of customers. The most obvious example is a web-based service. In general the site only has to be built once, but can service an increasing number of customers.

RESOURCE EFFICIENCY ISN'T SCALABILITY (NECESSARILY)

In my section on resource efficiency, I describe a framework that is helpful in understanding this investment criteria.

To clarify, I wanted to point out that resource efficiency is not necessarily synonymous with scalability. Scalability is often loosely used to describe how large a company can become. Both linear and exponential growth companies can become large businesses.

If scalability is used in reference to the economies of scale realized by a company, however, a more appropriate comparison may be drawn. Exponential growth companies generally have greater economies of scale, as variable costs are lower.

WHAT RESOURCE EFFICIENCY MEANS TO VCS

Both linear and exponential growth companies can become big businesses.

Some VCs will not invest in linear growth businesses. In general, the smaller the VC fund, the more inclined the partners are to avoid linear growth businesses. There is good reason for this. If a linear growth company requires a substantial amount of capital, VCs with small- to medium- sized funds are faced with either the prospect of substantial future dilution, limiting the investor's potential return, or overexposing their portfolio to a single company.

There are funds that do back linear growth companies. Generally, these are the funds with significant assets under management, making them large enough to support a linear growth company while avoiding dilution and portfolio imbalance.

Ultimately, understanding your company's resource efficiency will help you target the right investors.

Handling Getting Dinged

AVOID UNNECESSARY VC BASHING

VCs need to reject the vast majority of entrepreneurs who submit plans in order to do their job well. Nobody likes this – not the entrepreneur and not the

VC (especially VCs with entrepreneurial DNA). It's just part of the job.

While being rejected by a VC can be frustrating for entrepreneurs who passionately believe in their vision, it is important to handle the situation gracefully. The first step toward the right response is not to take the decision personally. VCs pass on investment opportunities for a variety of reasons, many of which are not a reflection of the concept or the entrepreneur.

Regardless of how you feel about the outcome of your fundraising process with an investor, it is important not to seek revenge by sullying the reputation of the VC without good reason. I write "without good reason." I am not attempting to advise entrepreneurs who dealt with a VC who did something truly inappropriate or unethical, such as lying or otherwise. In the absence of extreme situations, however, it behooves entrepreneurs to avoid saying bad things about VCs verbally or digitally.

At first read, this recommendation might appear to be self-interested. The reason I am offering this advice is not to protect VCs from a little criticism; I am writing this to help entrepreneurs avoid an unnecessary pitfall.

Yes, saying bad things about VCs can hurt entrepreneurs. Here's why: In order to be successful, a VC needs to know and meet with lots of entrepreneurs and other members of the venture community. As a result, VCs are generally relatively integrated across the seemingly large and disparate entrepreneurial community. What is six degrees of separation to many is just two or three degrees for VCs. Since they are typically well-networked, VCs hear lots of the rumors in the market; if word gets around it usually gets to investors.

This could potentially create two problems for an entrepreneur. First, if word gets back to the VC it might create bad blood, and they might return the favor of giving an entrepreneur a negative recommendation. Second, other VCs might hear about this, making them wary of interacting with the entrepreneur.

At the end of the day, the same rules that applied in high school apply in the venture community. Avoiding pettiness and unnecessary negativity is generally the best approach. Bad karma has a way of finding its way back to its creator.

DON'T TRY TO FORCE FIT YOUR MODEL INTO A VC'S THESIS

The challenge in the fundraising process is in the matching. Each VC is looking for something different and it's usually difficult for entrepreneurs to figure out what a VC wants before presenting to him.

What differentiates a VC's thesis is often far more nuanced than simply stage or sector. For example, within IT, some VCs are looking for companies that benefit from network effects, others want protectable technologies and others think a strong management team is the best barrier. Most funds would like to see all these characteristics, of course, but each makes different trade-offs when the time comes to make an investment decision. Ultimately, each VC fund differs in terms of what they need to see in an investment opportunity before it gets to "yes."

The nuances of these strategies lead funds to pass even on opportunities that align with their high level thesis: sector and stage. This can surprise entrepreneurs, frustrating those with high hopes.

As a result, when some entrepreneurs hear the unfortunate news, they try to fit in. Usually, doing so means making new claims about a fundamental characteristic of a business – often a characteristic that cannot be changed without revamping the entire business model. More often than not, this repositioning is not possible.

This tactic doesn't work very well. VCs will see through this change immediately, leading the entrepreneur to lose credibility with the VC and potentially impacting the VC's willingness to help the entrepreneur now or in the future. In the rare situations in which the VC doesn't sort this out immediately, he will over the coming weeks of meetings and diligence. Ultimately, this will lead to a waste of the VC's and the entrepreneur's time.

The best approach to fundraising is one in which entrepreneurs present their businesses as they actually are and continue to shop them around until they find a fit. Entrepreneurs who do this not only navigate the fundraising process more efficiently, but also gain the respect of the investment community along the way.

It is important to understand this nuanced aspect of VC investment strategies before starting the fundraising process.

ARTIFICIALLY REPOSITIONING VS. EVOLVING

To highlight the importance of not artificially repositioning a business plan in order raise capital from VCs, I want to offer some additional color. There is an important distinction between artificially repositioning a business and genuinely evolving the business plan.

By artificial repositioning, I refer to making unrealistic claims about the business. For example, after hearing that an addressable market size is not large enough to meet a VC's investment criteria, claiming that the addressable market size is actually much larger than previously stated (without a new plan to sell to new customer groups) is disingenuous. In situations like these, the underlying business plan has not changed – just its positioning.

If, however, after management was told that its addressable market was too small for the VC's needs, the management team then identified a new customer segment to target, it would be reasonable for the team to come back to the VC pointing to a larger addressable market. This is an example of a management team evolving in response to feedback. Not only does the evolution of a plan justify a new discussion with the VC, but constant, thoughtful reimagining of a business is also a good thing early in the life of a company.

It's worth noting that some models cannot evolve to meet the requirements of a specific investor. For example, some VCs don't invest in hardware-dependent businesses. If an entrepreneur pitches a business that is dependent on hardware to such a VC, it might be impossible for this company to ever meet the investor's thesis.

At the end of the day, there is an important distinction between artificial repositioning and evolving a strategy. If you can evolve the company (and like the new model), do so. If you can't, don't try to artificially reposition the company – it will do more harm than good.

ENTREPRENEURS SHOULD ASK

When VCs let entrepreneurs know they are not going to invite them in for a first meeting (after having reviewed the executive summary), the VC often provides little in the way of an explanation. This is partly because they are busy and partly because they want to avoid saying negative things about your idea. VCs understand that entrepreneurs love their brainchild just like a child.

Entrepreneurs who receive vague rejection emails should ask why. The VC's rationale for passing can be very useful to you for learning how people perceive your business. This feedback from VCs can help you understand which criteria your company did not meet, which is extremely valuable. If the VCs thought it was a bad business idea, you may want to re-evaluate your idea. If they passed because your company is not a good investment opportunity, you may need to look for alternative ways to finance your venture. If the VC liked the company but felt it was misaligned with their investment strategy, you should refine the list of VCs that you are targeting.

When you ask for feedback, remember to be polite. If a VC continues to be provide vague responses, stop bothering them and move on. Harassing a VC for feedback is not going to help you. Annoying them will not compel them to provide insight and it could give you a bad reputation.

While it's easier to avoid asking for feedback that is likely to be negative, entrepreneurs are better off asking. Check your pride and try to learn from every step in the VC process – it will make you a better entrepreneur and increase your chances of finding and convincing the right VCs to invest.

WHY VCS MAY NOT SHARE INSIGHTS

When VCs tell you that they're not interested, they may provide you with little insight about why they turned you down. The level of transparency provided in the rejection email varies based on both the VC's personal style and tactical considerations.

With regard to style, some VCs are less direct than others. As a result, they may avoid a direct explanation to be polite. They may also feel a need to hold their tongue if you were referred by a friend or important business contact. VCs know that most entrepreneurs take VC feedback personally.

There's also another key issue; giving feedback can be time consuming. Not only does it take time to craft a thoughtful email, but they often lead entrepreneurs to reply with more information or ask questions. Entrepreneurs often view feedback as an invitation to engage in a dialogue. Unfortunately, VCs don't have time to engage in dialogues with thousands of entrepreneurs.

If a VC doesn't provide sufficient feedback, ask for it and then just listen. Once you are done listening, if you feel you could refute the VC's stated reasons for rejection, ask if the VC would be willing to hear your arguments. The answer might be no. That doesn't mean the VC isn't open to your points, but it may mean he's aware of them and/or has other reasons for rejecting that he's decided not to share.

THE FIRST MEETING

What to Do in the First Meeting

WHOM YOU SHOULD BRING TO YOUR FIRST MEETING

Figuring out whom to bring to your first meeting is very important. You need to make sure that you bring members of your leadership team who will help you achieve your objective.

It's important that the people responsible for figuring out the "what" and the "how" are there. The person answering the "what" is usually the visionary who developed the concept for the business. The person addressing the "how" is often the CEO. If not, the CEO should come as well.

In an early stage company it's frequently the case that one person is answering both the "what" and the "how." But if there is only one person leading the charge, it's worthwhile to bring along the second most senior person (e.g., head of development), as VCs want to learn about your team's compatibility.

However, bringing too many people can also be problematic. VC teams usually allocate one or two people to a deal in order to spread their available man-hours across a lot of deals. As a result, you will usually only be meeting with one or two VCs. If you bring four or more people to the meeting it can create an awkward dynamic; it might seem like you are trying to intimidate the VC through numbers (which you won't) and it dilutes the intimacy of the interaction, limiting your ability to develop the relationship with the VC.

As the business becomes more mature, you will likely feel compelled to bring more people as there is more to talk about. However, if you bring too many people from your bench, you're probably trying to do too much in the first meeting.

In sum, you should bring two or three people to the meeting, unless you really need more than that to explain the "what" and the "how."

SIT ON ONE SIDE OF THE TABLE

When your team arrives at the VC's boardroom, you should all sit on the same side of the table. There are several reasons for this:

1. This enables the VCs to face your team, avoiding kinking their necks.
2. Having people surrounding a VC makes it feel like your group is trying to intimidate them. This sends the wrong message.
3. This is an unsaid etiquette; failure to understand this is an indication that your team may not be competent enough to form future business relationships.

If your team is too big to fit on one side of the table, you brought too many people. Sit together. It will make your team appear unified and thoughtful.

THE OBJECTIVE OF THE FIRST MEETING

The purpose of the first meeting with a VC is to get a second meeting. The purpose of the first meeting is not:

- To secure an investment from the VC after the conclusion of that meeting, or
- To tell the VC everything there is to know about your company.

VCs are generally too busy to dive deeply into every business that they see. In the first meeting, the VC's primary objectives are:

- To verify that the high-level characteristics of your plan are realistic and based upon solid research and strategic thinking, and
- To further validate the fit between your business and the VC's investment criteria.

The high-level characteristics that a VC will be testing are the ones that you listed in your executive summary as well as the competency and compatibility of the management team. VCs test these characteristics by identifying critical assumptions in your pitch and asking you direct questions about these assumptions. VCs will listen to you explain the high-level characteristics of your plan and then take deep dives into specific aspects of this plan that either interest or trouble them. When they dig deeper into an aspect of your business, they are testing you. They want to know that you have thought your business through and done so correctly.

Keep your eye on the ball. Your objective in the first meeting is to help VCs get comfortable with the high-level aspects of your business. If the VCs believe your vision and if your business aligns with their investment strategy, they'll invite you back for a second meeting when you can provide more detail. Focus on crawling before walking – get the second meeting and you'll be on the road to being funded.

CHANGE ELEVATIONS: THE STRUCTURE OF A PRESENTATION

There is a coined phrase that I hear often: "The fifty thousand foot view." When an entrepreneur tells me that they now want to talk about the "fifty thousand foot perspective," it means that they want to describe the bigger picture, illustrating the greater significance of their plan and why this opportunity is so inherently exciting. Keeping with this language, it is important to change elevations throughout the course of a presentation.

When presenting your company, you'll need to help your investors understand the bigger story. That doesn't mean, however, that you should exclude the details of your plan. It is important to communicate the details of your model and how you intend to execute. Through the course of a meeting you should alternate between the fifty thousand foot view and getting down into the weeds.

While there is not a one-size-fits-all pattern for providing information in a meeting, there is a structure that usually seems to work. This is the same structure you learned in grade school – it's the structure of an essay. I was taught that essays should do the following: 1) tell the reader what you're going to tell them, 2) tell them and 3) tell them what you told them with some broader implications. The parallel for a presentation is:

1. Tell them what your business does (a mission statement) while highlighting why they will want to invest (through an investment overview slide). Stay at the fifty thousand foot level.

2. Tell them how you will make your mission statement and the elements of your investment overview slide come true. Get into the weeds here.
3. Tell them what you told them by coming back up to the fifty thousand foot level and add the big picture into the mix.

No two meetings will be the same as investors ask questions that steer you in various directions, but I find that entrepreneurs who use this structure have more successful meetings. It helps guide the investor through the plan. This general structure will enable you to set the bait and give structure to the meeting in the first segment, bring your investors up to speed on your plan in the second and, once they understand what you are trying to achieve, get them excited in the third.

HOW TO INTRODUCE YOURSELF

VCs often ask entrepreneurs to tell them a little bit about their background.

When a VC asks this question, they are looking for a high-level 30-second summary of your background. Start with your name and title in the company, then rattle off the companies, titles and one-liners for all of the steps in your career. "I was a VP at Pepsi, where I led the South American branding initiative," would be a good example of concise coverage for a segment of your experience. If VCs are intrigued about a specific topic or feel compelled to dive in, they will. You don't need to volunteer lots of extra color.

A VC asks entrepreneurs about their backgrounds in order to get a high-level sense of the likely skill-set of each team member to confirm that the group complements each other and is well-aligned with their respective roles. While this will also inform their sense of your competency, the interaction throughout the meeting will have more bearing.

It's worth practicing before the meeting to be sure that each member of your team is prepared to give their personal pitch before they arrive. Why practice? Two reasons.

First, the personal pitch can make some people feel uncomfortable; few like to be scrutinized and judged by other people. However, you have to be ready for this question and avoid letting your anxiety translate into excessive chatter.

Second, VCs might not provide a significant response to your personal pitch. Don't mistake their lack of nodding or questions as a call for more information – it's not. They are probably simply listening to your story and taking it in – digesting whatever you give them. If you enter the meeting expecting this response, the silence won't give you or your team as much anxiety.

SOLID TEAM INTRODUCTIONS EXPLAIN WHY A COMPANY WAS STARTED

It's often said that the best startups are founded by entrepreneurs who built the product for themselves. While that rule doesn't always hold true, I can say it's generally a good thing when entrepreneurs have deep domain expertise in the space where they are innovating.

Because of this, when the team is asked to introduce themselves, the best startup teams often dovetail into an explanation of why they started the company. For most entrepreneurs, there is a connection between where they came from and where they are going, but not every entrepreneur explains their background in this light. There is good reason, however, to weave your bio into a story of why you're starting this company:

- First, it helps explain why you're the right person to chase this business;
- Second, it helps provide you with credibility when you're explaining the dynamics of the market which you are about to enter;
- Third, it often makes for a more compelling story and a nice transition into the rest of your presentation.

Founders who handle this introduction well either explain how prior experiences unveiled this opportunity for innovation or illustrate how a common thread of interest or experience connects the phases of their life (from as early as childhood) to this venture.

Investors know that you need the right team for a given startup, so when you're explaining your background to them, be sure to highlight why your path, interests and broader story make you the right person to change your target sector.

COMPETITION: PROVIDE INSIGHT

After you set the stage for your company's competitive positioning with your investment overview slide, be prepared to take a deeper dive into the competitive landscape. More often than not, VCs won't know the competitive landscape for your marketplace off hand so be sure to have information about all of the existing competitors.

However, provide more insight than a mere list of other firms. All too often, entrepreneurs only provide a slide of competitor logos or a brief description of each company. While that's a helpful start, VCs also want to know how those companies are positioned relative to yours. Make sure that you explain why your model is better and how you're going to beat them. This will help VCs appreciate your business and it will demonstrate your effectiveness at communicating as a manager.

Also be sure to provide information about your competitors that will make it easy for VCs to conduct due diligence. VCs are going to do the diligence whether you make it easy for them or not. However, by making it easy, VCs will appreciate your ability to operate as a partner.

A great way to present your strategic positioning is through the use of a 2x2 matrix. These diagrams help investors understand how you are differentiated from the competition in terms of two key facets – which fortunately you get to choose.

Example 2x2 Matrix

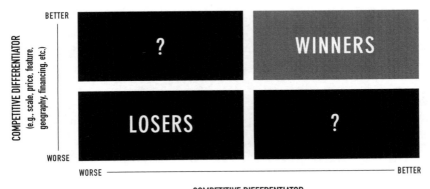

COMPETITIVE DIFFERENTIATOR
(e.g., scale, price, feature, geography, financing, etc.)

What VCs Will Be Watching For

MANAGEMENT COMPETENCY AND COMPATIBILITY

In your first meeting (and thereafter) a VC will be looking for two key qualities in your management team: competency and compatibility.

Your team can demonstrate competency in a few ways. The easiest is to have people on the team who have been successful entrepreneurs. However, you can demonstrate competency without being on your third startup.

The best way to do this is simply by being prepared. Know your industry, know your business model, have a clean presentation, know your barriers, know your competition, use an addressable market (not a market size) and appear comfortable with the information. When a VC sees this they will gain comfort with your team's ability.

Note that being prepared doesn't mean you need to have every answer. It's okay to not know some details offhand or to not have conducted an obscure analysis before the meeting. While it's no big deal to circle back on some of the questions a VC has, giving the wrong answer can destroy trust.

Perception can quickly influence reality. Be sure to demonstrate your team's competence by being prepared and being honest.

VCs will be looking for two types of compatibility in your team. First, they will want to see that you and your partners can work together. If you and your partners have a falling out during the infancy of the company, VCs could lose their investment. As a result, they want to see that you complement each other, work well together and have a relationship that will continue to function even when times get tough.

Second, VCs want to know that they are compatible with your team. A VC once said that the average length of both an investment and a marriage is seven years. By investing in your company, VCs are committing to spend a lot of time with you. If you can't make nice, you probably won't get funding.

ENLISTING YOUR COMPLEMENTS

VCs are looking for this balance between understanding and specialization in management teams. CEOs don't need to be functional in the CTO role, but it's very helpful when they can understand what a CTO is doing, what the challenges and opportunities the CTO faces and ultimately how they can help the CTO. Note that the level of understanding required to identify opportunities and be helpful likely varies by the technical complexity of the product.

While having an understanding of other people's roles is important, the CEO should also be careful not to invest too much time in understanding the CTO's work. Time is a finite resource and the CEO needs to be focused on CEO activities.

You don't need to have all of the skills required to run the entire company by yourself. Nobody is Superman. The key is to recruit partners and employees who complement the areas where you are not strong. It's the collective skill set of the management team that counts.

GOOD MANAGEMENT TAKES LESS TIME

I mentioned previously that VCs select good management because they will be fun to work with and can get the job done. However, there is another benefit to backing great management teams: they require less hand-holding. It's worth noting this, as it further explains VC focus on management teams.

To clarify, good VCs are willing to give entrepreneurs and the company the support they need. However, the best management teams typically don't need as much attention.

The reason that the second-tier management teams need more time is because they are unable to manage the most difficult situations that will inevitably arise from a startup. While they generally do the right thing in these situations and reach out to their board for advice, this creates more work for VCs. The best managers are able to handle these situations independently, often reducing board contact from requests for help to updates.

In addition, second-tier managers can become the crisis. Big egos can create dramatic demands and poor managers may force the board to find their replacement. Either scenario can create lots of stress and work for the board.

With this in mind, take an honest look at your team and make the extra effort to fill any gaps with the absolute best people available.

CONCERNS ABOUT SUCCESSFUL ENTREPRENEURS

VCs generally get excited about backing entrepreneurs that have successfully exited a venture. However, the stereotype of the repeat entrepreneur brings with it a concern.

Good VCs expect repeat entrepreneurs to act as partners, as they do everyone else. However, first-time entrepreneurs or entrepreneurs who have failed in prior endeavors are known for being more receptive to feedback and willing to engage in a healthy exchange of ideas. Repeat successful entrepreneurs are expected to be more stubborn, because they haven't experienced a humbling business endeavor yet.

As a result, repeat successful entrepreneurs should be sure to show VCs that they are team players. The best way to do this is by being friendly in the meeting and by being receptive to feedback. If you immediately dismiss a VC's reaction to your business plan, they'll assume that you'll dismiss them as board members in the future.

VCs are sensitive to this issue. Go the extra mile to demonstrate that this won't be a problem, and it will be even easier for you to get the deal done.

BUILD RAPPORT

It's important that you build the right type of rapport with VCs. However, it's hard for many first-time entrepreneurs to figure out what type of relationship they should have with VCs. Should you be deferential, bossy or a cold professional?

The answer is, none of the above. It's a bad idea to be too differential or to be overly complimentary. Those tactics are transparent, seem calculated and ultimately make people uncomfortable. Similarly, being bossy will offend VCs and being cold will make you a less desirable person to work with.

Ideally, your relationship with a VC should be that of a partner. Treat the VCs how you would treat a respected business partner. Be polite, friendly and responsive. This doesn't mean that you shouldn't challenge their assumptions and engage in debate – just do it as you would with a business partner. You should also get to know them. Building the relationship a little beyond the business world will make working together easier in the future.

At the end of the day, the compatibility of your team is a factor in the investment decision. The best way to be compatible is to be is treat VCs like a future partner.

VC Presentation Tips

PITCH IS NOT THE RIGHT WORD

It's common to call a presentation to a VC a "pitch". There are lots of phrases that make us use this word (elevator pitch, pitch book, etc.) and I am guilty of using it myself. However, it's not really the best way to describe what an entrepreneur should be doing.

The word pitch implies salesmanship – an attempt to convince a VC that your idea is exceptional. That's not the right approach. You shouldn't be trying to sell VCs on your concept; the facts should sell themselves. Your job is to educate the VC on the plan and the vision – there's no need to exaggerate.

The problem with overselling a concept is that a VC is going to eventually kick the tires. It will make you look bad if the hub caps fall off. You'll lose the trust of the VC, someone you should want to be your partner throughout the life of this venture and your future endeavors.

The opposite extreme, underselling, should be avoided as well. Not overselling doesn't mean hiding enthusiasm or underselling the facts. Share your passion for your idea; VCs do need to see that to believe in your commitment to the company. This shouldn't be a dry presentation, just an honest one.

Often the most technically capable managers undersell the opportunity. They want to highlight the point that their projections are attractive even when conservative. This approach can be helpful. However, some key metrics are most useful when they are accurate, not understated. For example, it's unfortunate when an addressable market is intentionally estimated to be too small – the VC has to invest their time calculating the real opportunity.

It's not a pitch; it's a presentation of the facts. It's why your team is the horse to bet on and why you are excited to pursue this venture. Provide the most accurate story that you can and you'll earn the trust and respect you'll need to be successful.

PROPRIETARY LINGO CAN CONFUSE INVESTORS

Entrepreneurs often create new lingo to describe the novel elements of their business. They do this for good reason – it's difficult to describe new ideas with old terminology. If a new concept takes numerous words to describe every time it comes up, you can bet that new labels and a new lexicon will be created to make conversation easier.

Developing this lingo is a good thing as it helps:

- Facilitate communication about these new ideas, and
- Creates a culture around the product. New terminology has a great way of making products seems special or unique.

A challenge arises when this lingo is used in investor pitches without explanation. Generally, I think including this lingo in the fundraising process is a good thing as it shows marketing savvy and gives investors more of a sense that the product is truly original. The key to using lingo successfully is to be sure to:

- Only use lingo where it's needed (if there is existing language for an idea, use the original concept), and
- Take the time to define the lingo.

I have found that many entrepreneurs struggle to clearly define the terms that they're using. Since to them the new word represents a concept, their explanations are often very abstract, further confusing the matter. To define them effectively, however, these new words need to be explained in a context that investors can understand. If the new product is a technology product, for example (e.g., Twitter's "tweets"), the entrepreneur should be careful to explain the product in its most basic form. For example, one might describe a tweet as a 140-character message sent to anyone following the author.

If you have catchy lingo for your new product, be sure to test it on your friends. If they don't get it, try explaining it differently.

WHAT IS A DESIRABLE OUTCOME?

VCs often ask entrepreneurs the question: "What's a desirable outcome for your startup?" While this question might be posed in different ways (e.g., "What are your goals? or "Where do you see this company going?'), all of these questions are a way of assessing your ultimate objective for your startup. Ultimately, these questions are a VC's way of testing the extent to which your objectives are aligned with those of the VC.

Entrepreneurs might have a number of different objectives. Three of the most common are:

1. An exit that provides significant cash to the entrepreneur, but not necessarily a huge exit in the scheme of things,
2. To build a big company and take it public or sell it for a large value, or
3. To run a company.

The first answer is usually a red flag to VCs, as it means there could be internal strife in the future if the board passes up an opportunity for a small exit. In contrast, an entrepreneur seeking a big exit is always music to a VC's ears.

The third response requires further analysis. While VCs like to back an entrepreneur who seeks to take his company public but is willing to sell the company for the right price along the way, they are less comfortable backing entrepreneurs who aim to avoid liquidity events (sale of the company or IPO). The latter scenario usually manifests itself in entrepreneurs who are motivated by the idea of sitting at the top of a big company rather than by financial reward. This mindset is a red flag to VCs who want to have the support of the founders if there is an opportunity to accept an attractive exit offer or an opportunity to go public.

Ultimately, VCs want to know that you are seeking the same type of exit they are. If you have the same objectives as the VC (a big exit or an eventual IPO), then tell them so. If you are seeking a small exit or no exit at all, then you probably shouldn't be speaking to VCs in the first place.

PROVING YOU CAN EXECUTE

The objective of your first meeting with a VC is to generate enough initial interest to get a partner to learn more. To do this, you have to convince VCs that you are more than a competent manager; they ultimately want to know that you are ready to translate your vision into a business. Demonstrating this early on can mean the difference between gaining momentum and losing it.

Proving you can execute is something that you show, not tell. Therefore, a VC is not going to ask, "Are you prepared to execute?" Instead, you are going to hear one word over and over: "How."

How will you build the site? How will you acquire customers? How will you advertise? How? How? How? "How" will often be accompanied its good friend "many."

How many programmers do you need? How many sales reps will you hire? How many geographies will you target initially? How many partnerships will you acquire? How many months until launch? How many? How many? How many?

Be prepared to explain all of the details behind how you are going to create this company, but at this stage, only offer information beyond the top level when specifically asked. Otherwise you could get caught up in details and not accomplish your goal of having the VCs buy into the bigger picture and want to put time in to learn more.

Knowing the answers to the "how" questions will not only help you ace the meeting, but also ensure that you are indeed ready to launch your venture.

FIGURING OUT THE "HOW"

As explained, when presenting to VCs, it is important to be able answer the questions about how you are going to execute. Finding the right answers is often difficult.

Part of the answers show that you are already building the business, which is what you should be doing anyway. What you are currently doing should provide a VC with guidance about the method for achieving your objectives and demonstrate your ability to figure out what needs to be done. For example, if asked, "How will you acquire customers," the best answer is a description of how you have acquired your first customers. If a lack of funding or product or talent keeps you from signing your first customers, get as close as you can to doing so – talk to potential customers, draft contracts to be signed once you meet some hurdle the customer has laid out for you, and so on. If you are doing all you can to develop the business without VC funding, answering part of the how questions should be easy.

The other part of the answer will come from your plan to execute after funding comes in.

The best answer to a how question about your use of resources after funding is rarely as many as possible. As an entrepreneur, you will always have limited resources. The answers to the "how" are the product of a resource balancing act.

For example, you might need sales reps, a marketing budget and a development team. Figuring out how much capital and time to invest in each may not be easy, since they all could be mission critical.

The best way to formulate a sophisticated resource allocation plan is through operational and financial modeling. If someone on your team knows how to do this, you should be in good shape. If not, you should recruit someone who does. You need to find your team's complement.

People who have worked in strategy consulting or in business development are usually well suited for this role. If you are having trouble finding someone, make sure to look at local business schools.

GIVE STRAIGHT TALK

VCs are going to ask you tough questions in the meeting. The answers to some of the questions may not present aspects of your business in the best light. As a result, lots of entrepreneurs try to dodge these questions. That's a bad idea.

When an entrepreneur tries to dodge a question, VCs know it and it makes them suspicious about the plan and the management.

- It makes VCs think they found the Achilles heel of the business plan, and
- It makes them think the entrepreneur is not going to be an honest partner in the future.

Attempting to dodge questions isn't worthwhile. Most business plans have some riskier aspects – VCs expect this. There are three reasons it benefits entrepreneurs to be open about these weaknesses:

1. Trying to hide them is a waste of everyone's time; VCs are going to spend weeks to months thinking about your business. They'll find them eventually,
2. VCs may be able to help fortify these weak points in the plans, and
3. You want to build an honest relationship with a VC so that they will feel compelled to work with you on this and future endeavors. Being open about weaknesses will foster this relationship.

For these reasons, you should answer all questions directly, even ones with answers that are weaker than you would like. For example, if you do not yet have paying customers, when asked if you have paying customers, do not skirt the question with an answer like "We are in the midst of contract negotiations with Company A. We had a great meeting with them this morning ... "

Instead, say something like "No, we have not yet generated our first revenue, but are in contract negotiations with our first customers. Would you like to go through our sales pipeline?"

Be a straight shooter when you're speaking to VCs. It will help you develop the rapport that you need with a partner who can help you build your company.

EXPECT STRAIGHT TALK

In that first meeting (and at any other time) you should also expect straight talk from the VC. To be clear, by straight talk I mean blunt, direct and candid questions and comments.

The style of each VC varies a great deal. Straight talk from some VCs will be warm and friendly – from others it may seem harsh. However, few (if any) will want to waste time with indirect questions.

VCs use straight talk because they need to get answers to their questions rapidly in order to avoid wasting time on deals they ultimately won't invest in. Being direct makes the dialogue more efficient. It's not intended to be rude or offensive – just efficient.

They key is to be prepared. It often appears that a VCs direct line of questioning catches entrepreneurs off guard. They seem to feel attacked even when the meeting is going well.

Be prepared for this dynamic and don't take it personally. Don't let the pace of the conversation distract you from your objective.

PRESENT FLEXIBLY

In order to achieve your objective in this first meeting, to interest VCs in learning more, you should focus on providing the VCs with the information they need. Most entrepreneurs plan on imparting this information through their PowerPoint presentations.

When most entrepreneurs practice these presentations, they focus on smoothing out the pace of their talk. While it's good to practice and get comfortable with the content of your presentation, it's important to keep the order and pace flexible; I can guarantee that you won't go in the order or at the pace you expected.

You will need to adapt the pace of the presentation to the needs of the VC. They will initially be more interested in some aspects of the business than others. Let the VCs needs set the pace and the topics. This will help them get the information they need to evaluate the idea quickly and get excited enough to move the process forward.

Some of the best ways to figure out what a VC wants to learn about your company is by reading their body language, responding to verbal cues and, if necessary, soliciting questions. If a VC gives you a quizzical look, slow down and spend more time on the topic. If they look bored, speed up. If they say, "We get it, move on," then move on. And, be sure to stop occasionally to offer to answer questions.

Also let the VCs questions guide the presentation – try not to defer questions until you get to an upcoming slide. If the VC is hung up on a question, they're less likely to pay attention to other material until their burning question is answered. Don't fret if these questions take you down a new, unexpected tangent. The VC is simply trying to get the information that they need – your job is to help them learn.

In order to achieve your objective in the first meeting you need to be flexible in how you present. Remember that your objective is not to present as rehearsed, it's to properly inform the VC and move the process forward.

SOLVE THE VC'S ISSUES

In your first meeting, you need to solve the VC's big issues. It's likely that before (or during) the first meeting, the VC will have identified several key concerns that could end their interest in your venture. These could be the competitive threat, the addressable market size, the likelihood of acquiring partnerships or a variety of other topics.

In that first meeting, VCs will try to understand those topics well enough to determine whether or not to continue evaluating your company. It's usually pretty easy to figure out which issues the VC is most concerned about. Telltale signs include lots of questions about a topic and/or concerned facial expressions.

When you are managing the pace of your presentation, be sure to allocate more time to these topics. Make sure not to move on to other topics until you have done everything you can to get the VC on board with your perspective on these issues.

If you find that multiple VCs get hung up on the same issues and you can't convince them that their concerns do not present a significant challenge for the business, you should consider the possibility that they are right. This could be an indication that there is a problem with your current model. Take a step back and innovate – create a solution to the big issue before continuing to meet with other VCs.

If the problem is truly intractable, it may be that venture capital financing is not appropriate for your business. Many great businesses have been built without venture capital financing; venture capitalists focus on a specific type of investment opportunity, and a minority of private companies fit this profile.

You won't be able to get every VC to see your vision, but you should always do your best to solve each VC's big issues so they can get one step closer to believing.

TELL THE BIGGER STORY

I have found that entrepreneurs are told to not oversell their business when they meet with VCs. This advice is problematic because it often scares entrepreneurs away from selling the part of their idea that is exciting. There's a difference between selling and exaggerating; I will explain.

If you genuinely believe your business will generate $10 million of revenue in year three, then you shouldn't tell your investors that you'll do $25 million or $100 million in your third year. Be realistic and be honest.

The problem with this advice, however, is that it implies that you shouldn't tell a bigger story – the grand vision could come off as hyperbole or over-salesmanship. In my experience, the bigger picture is what makes a business really exciting. If phase one of the company can generate a decent-sized business, but phase two can create a behemoth, describe phase two – it only makes the opportunity better. Investors want to know how your business can become a giant.

If your intuition tells you that the bigger picture is a little more far-fetched and less believable given where your business is today – making you nervous about sharing the vision, just couch the bigger picture appropriately. For example, you might say, "In phase one, we're going to build this business, which we think can become a $100 million company. At that point we might be able to take the next step of X which could present a billion dollar opportunity." This approach allows you to sound reasonable, while still sharing the bigger picture.

While investors vary in what they are looking for, many early stage VCs are looking for companies that have a shot of realizing billion dollar valuations and in order to do that, there usually needs to be a bigger story. Not sharing that story can be doing yourself a disservice. Take a risk and paint the bigger picture.

What Not to do in the First Meeting

DO NOT READ FROM A SCRIPT

Not all CEOs are the charismatic leaders depicted in magazines. Charm alone doesn't make a good CEO. However, a minimum level of confidence and a base level of interpersonal skills are usually required for CEOs to be successful. If you are a founder who does not have these traits, simply bring someone onto the team who does. Find your complement.

One symptom that demonstrates a lack of core CEO skills is your ability to explain your business in your first meeting with a VC. If you find that you are so nervous that you need to write out all of your answers to every possible question in that meeting so that you can read your answers from a paper in the meeting, it is time to re-evaluate your role in the business.

To many, this suggestion may sound obvious. However, VCs see a large volume of presenters and this scenario happens from time to time. If you find yourself wanting to read from a script, be honest with yourself, figure out what your strengths are and find someone to help you. It's a misconception that you have to be the CEO to be successful. The key to success is playing to your strengths so that you are positioned to succeed.

DO NOT RAMBLE

One way entrepreneurs frequently get off track in their presentations is by trying to squeeze as much information as they can into the conversation, with the hope that some of the details will hook the VC.

It's important that you don't ramble in any of your interactions with a VC. VCs know you are rambling because of the reason listed above. As mentioned before, VCs don't need to hear every detail of your plan to make a decision. When VCs think an entrepreneur is trying to share their entire business plan in a phone call or first meeting, it makes the entrepreneur appear naive and inexperienced.

In the first meeting, focus on explaining the high-level characteristics of your plan and address specific questions posed by a VC. Extraneous information can take the conversation down a new tangent, clutter the big picture and ultimately prevent VCs from achieving their objective of sanity checking your high-level assumptions. Keep it simple – too much irrelevant information can result in you not being asked to another meeting.

DO NOT NAME DROP

The fact that name-dropping is a bad idea should go without saying, but a few entrepreneurs have proven the need for this section.

When you are presenting your business, it's a bad move to rely heavily on opinions of big name people in order to validate the quality of your idea. In other words, don't expect to sell the merits of your idea simply based on the opinion of a third party. Statements like "Bill Gates loves what I'm doing" are not very effective for a few reasons:

1. It raises questions about why Bill isn't backing you,
2. It sounds like a petty attempt to cover up the weaknesses of your plan, and
3. It sounds tacky, making people think that you are bad to be around.

That said, having the support of industry experts is a relevant factor for VCs to know. However, instead of demonstrating this through a quote, get them to join your advisory board or invest in your company. That's a real sign of faith.

Focus on explaining the merits of your business – those factors will speak louder than any names you can drop.

DO NOT INTERRUPT YOUR PARTNER

Continuing with the theme of compatibility, I wanted to address one aspect of presentation etiquette: interrupting your partners during a pitch to a VC. If a partner is speaking during a presentation, let him finish his thoughts. Cutting him off makes your team look bad and leads VCs to think:

1. That you guys can't coordinate well and do not make a highly functional team,
2. That you are desperate,
3. That you are going to interrupt VCs when they are on your board, and
4. That your team is not going to be effective at business development (it's not hard to imagine you interrupting each other in front of partners and customers).

One easy way to avoid appearing like a two-headed monster is to appoint one person to be the lead presenter. The secondary presenter should add important insights along the way, but not compete for air time.

This might seem like an obvious point, however, I see it happen frequently. This is an easy thing to avoid – so, do yourself a favor and be thoughtful about this.

DO NOT FOCUS ON THE EXIT

It's not uncommon for entrepreneurs to start talking about their exit strategy in detail during one of their first meetings with a VC. While it's generally a good idea to indicate your intention of eventually exiting, VCs do not want to hear that you believe you have figured out the exact timing and buyer. To clarify, VCs like to know that there are potential buyers in the market and that you intend to exit; they don't want to hear that you know who is going to buy you unless you have had serious discussions toward that end with the potential acquiring party.

VCs don't like to hear these speculations for a few reasons:

1. You should not be too focused on the exit; you should be focused on building a great company. Great companies are often attractive acquisition targets – the exit will take care of itself.
2. If there are numerous potential buyers, you seem naïve to think you know who will make the acquisition.
3. If there is only one potential buyer for your company (which is rarely the case), that circumstance presents a substantial risk that VCs won't like.

However, if you are asked about who might acquire your company, be prepared to answer that question. The best answers not only list potential acquirers, but include rationale for the acquisition and examples of similar purchases made by that company.

My guess is that entrepreneurs describe their detailed exit plan because they know VCs want to back entrepreneurs who intend to develop an exit strategy for their company. However, in your first round of fundraising, it's generally better to say something more open ended such as, "I hope to be acquired in three to five years by one of the many potential buyers, but am focused on building a great company which will have lots of options."

AVOID DOING MENTAL MATH

Even quant gurus can trip up when doing mental math while giving a presentation. As a result, it's a good idea to avoid setting yourself up to do complicated math during your initial meetings with VCs.

One of the best ways to avoid this situation is to have backup slides that detail the underlying math of key analysis, such as cost of goods sold or the addressable market size. I find that entrepreneurs get into trouble when they have a slide the presents a summarized version of the calculation. These summaries beg questions about the underlying inputs, leaving you to start doing mental math while in the hot seat.

To further avoid doing mental math, you may want to respond to questions about inputs with an offer to send the document that illustrates the calculation after the meeting. While in the rare case in which this offer doesn't quell the investor's request, you should be prepared to open the supporting documentation and explain the math. The need to navigate through supporting documents during a presentation of a high-level overview of your business, however, is unlikely.

BE CAREFUL ABOUT OVER-SELLING FUNDRAISING INTEREST

VCs will often ask entrepreneurs where they are in the process with other investors. While most entrepreneurs' first reaction is to promote their progress with other VCs to drum up more interest, I'm not convinced that is always the best approach.

When it comes to promoting your progress with other investors, you should give the investor a indications about what stage you're currently at in the process. Comments such as: "we're starting to do meetings with investors", "we're expecting a term sheet" and such can give investors sufficient guidance to enable them to plan their own process for evaluating your company.

Similar to the point I made about setting expectations about operating performance, however, you should carefully manage a VC's expectations about your ability to acquire other term sheets. If you tell a VC that you expect two term sheets in a week and you don't get them, the VC will wonder what about your business scared away the other investors. This could severely hurt your momentum.

How to End the Meeting

FOLLOW-UP ITEMS

During the meeting, VCs may ask you to send them some material after the meeting. When they make a request you should do two things:

1. Clarify when they need it by so that you don't delay their due diligence process – you want to keep the momentum going.
2. Take notes. It can be hard to remember all of the information requests while selling your company and you don't want to forget any items or timing, as it could make you look disorganized.

You should view follow-up items as an opportunity to do more than provide information – this process can keep your company on top of the VC's list, enabling you to maintain momentum. To build the most momentum from this process, you should make sure that:

- Your follow-up items are complete and delivered promptly.
- You offer to review the materials over a brief phone call or meeting.
- You ask if there is any other information that they want.

THE ALMOST END OF THE MEETING

In my experience, when VCs are done asking questions about your company, they will often offer to tell you a bit about their fund. They usually provide a relatively canned pitch that should give you an overview, including these three areas:

1. Investment criteria and thesis,
2. Organization, and
3. Value proposition to entrepreneurs.

Every VC differs in these, and this is your chance to understand the nuances that make this VC unique. Feel free to ask them to clarify any of these points.

After this pitch, use the time at the end of the meeting to ask thoughtful questions. This time is a great opportunity for an entrepreneur to learn a bit about a potential future partner. While you should be sensitive to the time constraints of the VC (as they should be to yours), feel free to spend some time asking the VC about the fund. I would recommend asking some of the following questions, if you don't already know the answer:

- What is your decision-making process?
- Roughly when should I expect to hear from you?
- Where are you in your current fund (e.g., how many more investments do you plan to make?)
- How much do you typically invest in a first investment?
- How much do you reserve for follow-on investments?
- Do you lead, follow, or both?

Also, feel free to ask for more detail about aspects of the fund's investment criteria, thesis or value proposition.

Although a discussion about the VC is a relatively common part of a first meeting with a VC, you may find VCs to be somewhat anxious to keep the conversation about them short. There are a lot of possible reasons for this; however, the most likely reasons are that they either are running out of time or have decided that they are not interested in investing and therefore want to use their time more productively. Either way, it's always good to leave the meeting on a friendly note, so I recommend following a VC's lead in these cases and wrapping up.

ASK THE VC ABOUT FOLLOW-ON INVESTING

One question that you should always try to ask is whether or not the VC typically makes follow-on investments in subsequent rounds. There are a couple reasons why this is important to do. First, having your existing investors provide additional capital in subsequent rounds can help you more easily meet your funding needs. In addition, when your existing investors invest in subsequent rounds it makes raising capital from new investors easier, as follow-on investments signal that investors continue to believe in the company's prospects. Finally, having investors communicate an intention to make follow-on investments early in the process can increase the odds of them doing so in the future. This conversation can set their expectations about continued involvement.

WHAT TO DO WHEN THE MEETING ENDS

Unless you have arranged to stay in the room after the meeting, it's best to clean up and leave the office relatively quickly. There are a few reasons for this. The two most important ones are:

1. Most VCs have small office spaces with only a few conference rooms. It can put them in a tough spot if you force them to ask you to leave for another meeting, as few VCs want to be rude.
2. They may want to quickly deliberate about your company before another meeting, but prefer to wait for you to leave the office.

Do not talk about the meeting until you have left the building, and talking outside of the VC's office is not a great idea either. You never know when you might bump into one of their partners in a hallway or on the elevator.

AFTER THE FIRST MEETING

What Happens Next

WHAT TO EXPECT AFTER THE FIRST MEETING

After you have had your first meeting, VCs may be slow to respond. There are a few reasons.

First, (while processes vary by VC fund) it often takes a VC a week or more to discuss your venture with their partners. Most venture firms hold their partner meetings on Mondays and they discuss new companies at those meetings. So, if you met with the VC on a Tuesday, it may take them a minimum of a week to respond. However, if the partner that you met with is out of the office the following Monday or if the Monday partner meeting is cut short due to extraneous factors, it may take two weeks or longer for the VC to discuss the opportunity with their partners. Ultimately, a few weeks of waiting time does not necessarily mean that a VC is not interested.

Another reason why VCs may be slow to respond is because they are conducting some preliminary due diligence. If they have one key question about your business that they believe can be answered easily, they might first try to find out the answer before following up with you. However, getting this answer can sometimes take a few weeks. For example, if the VC has a contact with expertise in the field of question, it may take some time to get in touch with that individual if they are on vacation or otherwise inaccessible. This process may seem especially slow if the VC starts the diligence process after waiting to discuss the idea at the partner meeting. Aside from the natural causes of delay, no response may also mean that there is a lack of VC interest. VCs are inundated with business plans and other managerial responsibilities. As a result, only businesses that they are very interested in gain the momentum required for thorough exploration. If the VC wasn't excited about your opportunity, even if it is a great business, your business may get lost in the shuffle. Only the companies that VCs are most excited about seem to continuously float to the top.

In sum, be patient after the first meeting. VCs will not move as quickly as you. However, you should do what you can to develop and maintain the interest of a VC so that they continue to evaluate your company.

READING VC INTEREST

If VCs don't offer feedback, you can try to assess their interest by reading other signals.

The interest of VCs in your company is usually easy to read. Their tone is the best subjective indication of interest and their frequency of communication with you is the best objective indication.

With regard to tone, some VCs show emotion more than others. VCs who show their emotions will usually demonstrate excitement or a lack of interest in their conversations and correspondences with you. With VCs who are less emotive, you will have to look for more subtle indications such as an appearance of satisfaction with your answers to questions.

With regard to frequency of communication, at a high level, more is better. If you receive one email or phone call from them per week, they are likely to be more interested than if you are not contacted at all. However, there are some exceptions to this rule of thumb. For example, if you have just presented to a VC, he may be interested in your company but not contact you immediately, as most firms have an internal process to undergo. On the other hand, a VC may contact you frequently to understand one part of your business that they are uncomfortable with. For example, if your addressable market estimate seems too high to the VC they may have several conversations with you in a one-week period to better understand this issue, because it is preventing him from getting excited about your company.

In the end, you will have to draw some conclusions based upon the signs you see both in a VC's tone and frequency of communication (in the context of their process).

HEAR FEEDBACK

The best indication of a VC's interest is direct feedback. While some VCs will offer this feedback without being prompted, you may have to ask others (and it is okay to ask). If a VC gives you feedback, listen to it. Don't hear what you want to hear, hear what they say, no matter how unpleasant it might be.

Be sure to listen carefully to what VCs say even if you believe that it contradicts their actions. Often entrepreneurs will ignore direct feedback because they have decided that other signals (e.g., body language) are more telling. This is a bad idea. Listen to what the VC says to you first and foremost.

Most VCs are too busy looking at lots of deals to play games. If they tell you that they are not interested, move on.

If you rationalize away what a VC told you, you may ultimately make bad decisions. First, if you don't listen to feedback, your expectations for receiving capital may be misaligned. This has obvious implications for adversely impacting decision-making. Second, if you don't listen to the VCs feedback, you may justify interactions with them that annoy them which could ultimately damage the relationship.

The key is to take direct feedback at face value. It will make your life easier.

RESPOND TO REQUESTS RELATIVELY QUICKLY

During the due diligence process, VCs will make numerous information requests (common requests can include financial models, market size analysis and competitive landscape). It's rare for entrepreneurs to have all of the materials on file at the time of request – entrepreneurs typically need to create missing materials. As a result, it usually takes entrepreneurs a few days to submit these docs. Typically, the quick responses come in 24 hours and the slow take a work week. However, on occasion entrepreneurs take several weeks to deliver the requested materials.

While I do understand how busy founders are building their companies, in my opinion entrepreneurs should try to respond to information requests within the next five business days. There are a few reasons for this:

1. Responding quickly can demonstrate your interest in working with the investor. Slow responses may imply that you are not serious about rais-

ing money or spending more of your time with other investors. Early stage investors typically have lots of companies in the pipe and they don't want to waste time on uninterested parties.

2. A quick response creates the perception that you have your act together and are aggressive enough to succeed as an entrepreneur.

3. A slower response may create the perception that you are having trouble finding data that supports your prior claims; being quick to respond can make you appear more trustworthy.

4. Responding quickly demonstrates that you understand how to best allocate your time — you should be doing the bare minimum for these requests and investing most of your time in building a great company.

It is worth noting that there are always reasonable exceptions to this guideline. If you're traveling or closing a partnership you should mention that to the VC and let them know when you think you will have the information to them.

Fundraising is a delicate process — the small things can make all of the difference.

If Interest is Not Immediate

WHY VCS DON'T ALWAYS CUT YOU LOOSE

Some VCs are genuinely bad at responding to entrepreneurs. However, even highly responsive VCs sometimes have companies that fall into the no man's land between being given a yes or a no.

VCs understand that this murky area is undesirable for entrepreneurs. They don't avoid being decisive to punish entrepreneurs. Rather, VCs do this because it's their best option.

Making investments in early stage companies is a difficult task. VCs not only need to see the vision of the entrepreneurs, but they also need to evaluate the potential of each strategy and team. Most of the time it's relatively obvious to a VC whether or not they are interested in a company. However, there are always some companies that meet a VC's criteria, but still leave the VC with a few hesitations.

VCs don't want to walk away from these opportunities, since they know that new information in the future could get them interested in making a decision. However, they're not ready to invest based on what they currently know. Therefore, VCs will monitor these companies with the hope that they are given a reason to set aside hesitations.

WHAT'S ENOUGH TRACTION

It's not uncommon for an investor to ask an entrepreneur to circle back when they have more traction. While this is a reasonable request from investors, it often leaves entrepreneurs wondering, what's enough traction?

It depends.

The level of adoption required to make a given investor comfortable varies from company to company and investor to investor. There are, however, some guidelines based upon the type of customer that the company is targeting.

- **Business-to-consumer or prosumer:** Investors want to see hockey stick adoption rates, which imply consistent or increasing growth rates on a percentage basis. Depending on the company, investors will vary in how many months they want to see that pattern of sustained growth before investing.

- **Business-to-small & medium business (SMBs):** For companies targeting SMB customers, investors want to believe that there is a validated, repeatable profitable marketing equation. The marketing equation is defined as the relationship between the customer lifetime value and the cost of acquisition. Put simply, investors want to know that a company can repeatedly acquire customers for $X and generate more than $X in gross profit from each customer. Depending on the business, investors will likely vary in how many customers they want to see profitably acquired.

- **Business-to-enterprise:** Enterprise sales target the most concentrated customer base generally permitting for the fewest customers to adopt before capital needs become most urgent. In these situations, investors generally seek adoption from a few customers and verbal suggestions of intent to purchase from others. Additionally, investors try to understand the length of the sales cycle, as longer sales cycles drive companies to need more capital to generate revenue as they must sustain their burn rates for the duration of those cycles. Again, the required number of customers adopting varies by the company and investor.

In sum, there are no hard-and-fast rules, but when an investor suggests that you obtain more traction it's because they still need to be convinced that your customers are going to adopt en masse.

WHAT TO DO WHEN YOUR COMPANY IS BEING MONITORED

Being followed on "monitored" status, meaning that the VC wants to watch your progress before making a more formal decision, is not the ideal outcome for entrepreneurs. But, it's better than being rejected. If you are in this situation, take it as a sign that investors see most of what you see.

There are two things that you should do in this situation to move the process forward. First, you should continue to pursue other investors. However, be careful not to oversell the interest of the VC that is monitoring your company, as this could hurt you.

Additionally, you should do your best to give the investor the information that they need to get to "yes." To do this, you first need to listen. If you understand what is giving the VC pause, you can try to overcome that concern by providing them with additional company information. For example, if a VC is concerned about consumer adoption of your product, you should acquire customers and share your performance with the VC.

Lastly, if you can adapt your business model to remove their concerns, that's another great solution. It will show them that you listen and can evolve.

Ultimately, be positive. This is usually a sign that you are onto something likely to be worthwhile.

FIND A CHAMPION

During or after the first meeting, you need to find one person at the VC firm to be your champion – the person who will promote your company inside the fund. Your champion should be the person who is most interested and most qualified to sell the deal internally.

Ideally, your champion shouldn't be too junior or too senior. Junior VCs generally have less ability to create momentum internally. Some senior VCs might not be as active in most investments, and therefore aren't ideal since they won't put as much effort into promoting your company. The best champions are the still-active and most senior investors.

More often then not, you will not have a choice. One partner will be interested or the fund will decide internally who is going to focus on your company. However, if you have the opportunity to select your champion, pick wisely.

You will know if you are given the chance to select your champion because you will have a few points of contact at the firm. You pick one simply by communicating most frequently with that person.

When you identify your champion, you need to harvest the relationship by building and maintaining momentum.

HOW VCS MAKE DECISIONS INTERNALLY

While no two VC firms make decisions the same way, there are a few models that have developed based upon several constraining factors.

In an ideal world, every partner at a VC fund would spend considerable time evaluating each startup in which they invest. This would enable the fund to benefit from the diverse perspectives and experiences that the various members of the partnership bring to bear, ultimately enabling the partnership to make better investment decisions.

However, evaluating a business takes a lot of time and is an accretive process. As a partner learns more about a company, they are more likely to uncover investment risks. As a result, it is critical for there to be continuity in the due diligence process – the same person digging deeper and deeper. If every partner were trying to become a specialist on the same company, the firm wouldn't be able to evaluate many companies.

Given all of this, in a world where the only goal is to make the absolute best investment decisions every time, it would be optimal for every partner of a VC fund to focus all of their time on the same deal until they are ready to invest. Unfortunately, that's not realistic because each venture fund needs to deploy a target amount of capital in a given time period in order to meet their investor's expectations. In order to meet these expectations, partnerships collectively need to evaluate numerous businesses at any given time. In order to make enough high quality investments in a given time period, firms divide and conquer.

This dynamic has led to the creation of a few different decision-making models, which I describe below. It is worth noting that not every fund's decision-making model will fit cleanly into one of these categories, however, this framework should give entrepreneurs a way to think about how a fund's decisions are made.

The Union

In small firms (typically no more than five partners), one partner will lead the due diligence effort, but provide frequent updates about their findings to help all of the partners remain relatively knowledgeable about the deal as the lead partner learns more. When the due diligence phase is complete, the partnership requires a unanimous (or close to unanimous) vote to approve investment.

> Pros: This model enables the partnership to leverage the diverse experience of the partners to make better decisions.

Cons: This requires a significant amount of time from the partners who are not leading the due diligence effort.

The Federacy

Firms that are too large to use the consensus model, because it is too time consuming to keep all of the partners up to speed, may opt to give individual partners decision-making power. While the partners inevitably leverage the advice of each other, they have more autonomy in making their own decisions.

Pros: This enables larger partnerships to operate dynamically, making decisions more quickly with fewer man-hours.

Cons: The value of the diverse experiences of the partnership is not fully leveraged, as few of the partners have spent a significant amount of time evaluating each investment.

The Democracy

Some larger firms try to maintain a consensus model, whereby a voting mechanism is used to make decisions. However, unlike the Union model in small firms, partners who are not leading the due diligence effort typically know less about the business opportunity in larger partnerships. Rather than being tangentially involved in the due diligence process, non-lead partners rely on a presentation from the lead-partner to determine whether or not they want to make an investment.

Pros: This enables the wisdom of the group to be tapped when it's time to vote.

Cons: The firm's investment strategy tends to become less risky, which can lead to missing some of the more cutting edge opportunities. It typically takes longer to fully understand the value proposition and business model underlying some of the more cutting edge companies. As a result, a relatively short presentation of the company may not be sufficient to sell partners who have not been thinking about the business for several weeks.

HOW TO TAKE ADVANTAGE OF THE VC DECISION-MAKING PROCESS

As an entrepreneur, you should try to understand each VC's decision-making process as soon as you can. The best way to figure this out is to simply ask your contact how their process works.

If the VC fund uses a Federalist model, the process should be straightforward. Focus on generating interest with the partner who is your primary contact. However, if the VC fund uses a Union or Democracy decision-making process, you will need to try to get most or all of the fund's partners excited about your company. In order to do this you should be prepared to repeat your high-level pitch as you meet with new partners – don't assume that your primary contact has done your pitch justice when talking to other partners. Another key tactic you should employ is sending frequent materials and email updates along that your primary contact can forward to the rest of the partnership. This can help generate curiosity, if not interest.

While your tactics for creating interest in Union and Democracy partnerships will likely be similar, your access to the partners may vary considerably. In a fund that uses a Union process, your contact has an incentive to have all of his partners meet with you. In a Democracy, there may be too many partners for that to be realistic. As a result, you will need to make more of an effort to get mindshare from other partners.

One tactic that you should consider using in a Democracy environment is gently asking your lead partner if there are other members of the partnership that you should present to. Usually, this works best if you ask to present to specific partners whom you have identified as having relevant experience in your space. However, if you employ this tactic, do it delicately and be careful not to appear as though you want to go above your primary contact. There are probably politics within the partnership that you don't know about, so be sure to make the lead partner feel comfortable that they are driving the process of socializing your business within the firm. This tactic should be poised as a subtle question (for example, say "Do you think it would be helpful for John to take a look at our business given his experience in the sector?"), nothing more.

It's worthwhile to understand the decision-making process early, as this context will help you more effectively engage the partnership.

VCS ARE NOT LIKE YOUR PARENTS

Once in a blue moon an entrepreneur will try to play partners at a venture firm against each other – much like a child plays his mom against his dad.

The strategy used by a child is as follows. The child will ask his mom if he can have a candy bar. If he is told no, he asks his dad. The hope is that the second request will be approved. If mom said no and dad said yes the child can try to create controversy with the hopes of ultimately getting his treat.

The common parenting wisdom suggests that parents always offer the same answer, either yes or no; they should act in concert. Partners at a venture fund also follow this wisdom. You should assume that whatever response you get from one partner reflects the will of the entire firm.

In fact, it is rare that the response you receive is not the collective decision of the firm. One of the most valuable aspects of a partnership is that it allows VCs with different viewpoints to talk through many of the difficult decisions they confront. VCs spend a lot of time talking about companies with their partners. However, even in the less common case where a VC acts autonomously, the partnership will likely support that viewpoint. As a result, you should always assume that each VC has the whole firm behind him.

Trying to play one partner against each other, or trying to talk to several partners independently is a bad strategy. Here are a few reasons why:

1. It doesn't work. Partners frequently have casual conversations about their deals throughout the week and most firms review a pipeline document every Monday at their partner meeting. As a result, they will uncover your tactics very early in the process.
2. When they figure it out, it will make you look bad, as this tactic is both naive and a bit underhanded.

Ultimately, it's always best to be honest and open with VCs so that they feel you can be trusted as a partner going forward.

CREATING MOMENTUM

While some VCs have a very structured process for responding to entrepreneurs, others do not. I have said that VCs with less structured processes may not respond to you after your first meeting because of a lack of interest.

There are things you can do to increase their interest and add momentum to the process after the first meeting. These tactics are also relevant when a VC is interested in your company, as they will enable you to further increase momentum and further improve your likelihood of receiving an investment.

Before I dive into what you can do to create momentum, I want to reemphasize that this is a critical part of the process. A VC has to learn a lot about your company before they will make an investment. As a result, if a VC isn't moving through the evaluation process rapidly it could take a long time for them to decide to invest, leaving more opportunity for them to become distracted by another opportunity. Creating momentum is ultimately achieved by maintaining consistent periodic communication with the VC. Checking in can create the perception that there is some urgency and a real process in place (with them and the other VCs you may be talking too). The more there is a process in place the more likely they are to move quickly.

If there is nothing compelling them to move faster, they usually won't since taking longer to evaluate a deal can provide them with more information about your ability to execute (e.g., growth and performance), reducing the riskiness of the investment. Here are the tactics:

- When you check in and ask for the next step, be sure to listen to the answer. If you don't listen to them, you will frustrate them and damage the relationship.

- When you periodically provide the VC with relevant market research it will help them understand and get excited about the opportunity. Frequent touch points can keep you top of mind.

- Be strategic about how much information you send and when you send it. If you send all of your market research and news to a VC in one email, you won't have an excuse to reach out to them again in the future.

- Periodically notify the VC of your progress. Sending an occasional email with an update on newsworthy progress, such as partnerships, new hires, product development, favorable press, etc. can help the VC see your ability to execute and can help the VC become both more interested in you as a manager and more comfortable with the viability of your company.

With all of your outreach, be sure not to be annoying. Reaching out more than once or twice a week can make the VC not want to work with you since you are demonstrating a lack of awareness about boundaries.

One other thing to be aware of is that you can't always create momentum. If the VC has told you that they are not interested, you need to listen to that response and leave them alone. Continuing to harass them will only damage the relationship, limiting your ability to work with them in the future.

MAINTAINING MOMENTUM: CREATE URGENCY

Getting the VC to invest requires that the deal evaluation process maintain positive momentum. Maintaining momentum can be achieved by the periodic contact strategy I just described. However, another important tactic should also be leveraged to maintain momentum – the creation of urgency.

The best way to create urgency is to have competitive interest in your deal. You should reinforce this urgency by creating a deadline based upon progress you are making with other venture capitalists. This can be achieved by tying your time-tables to expected milestones with other VCs, such as term sheet timelines.

You should never lie about your other VC relationships. The venture community is very small and it is possible that VCs may speak to each other. Being caught in a lie could kill your credibility and, as a result, kill the deal.

The second best way to create urgency is through deadlines created by exogenous factors, such as a need for capital in order to continue executing against your plan. You can do this by making the case for why you need the capital according to a specific schedule. Be sure that this date is reasonable for the VC – you don't want them to feel that they shouldn't evaluate your company because they won't have sufficient time to complete their diligence. This suggests that you should carefully plan the timing of your fundraising process.

Regardless of the tactic that you use, be sure that you create urgency, not desperation. Creating perceptions of financial and operating needs as a tactic to create momentum can backfire, by making the VC think that you are 1) not in a good negotiating position, 2) not operating a viable business or 3) not capable of managing your business well, since you mistimed your fundraising. Any such interpretation hurts you.

Your Next Moves

IF YOU CAN'T CREATE INTEREST, MOVE ON

Sometimes, efforts to create momentum within a firm won't work because a VC has insurmountable concerns about your business. In these cases you need to gracefully move on.

Note that you may need to move on even if the VC has not formally said no. Ideally, VCs will let you know when they're not interested. However, if there is no momentum and conversations die out over time, then you should read the writing on the wall and move on.

To emphasize – when you move on, be graceful about it. When I say graceful, I mean two things: be polite in accepting their decision (stated or implied) and don't harass them if you disagree. There are two major reasons to take this approach.

The first reason is simply because it's the considerate and good thing to do. Put yourself in a VC's shoes for a minute. As part of the job, a VC must reject hundreds of entrepreneurs each year. They don't take pleasure in this and they're not doing it to "get you." They pass on business ideas because it is their fiduciary responsibility to allocate capital to the opportunities 1) that are consistent with the investment strategy that they described to their investors and 2) that they expect to generate the best returns.

That said, VCs understand that entrepreneurs are ambitious and have an obligation to their investors and teams to do their best to raise venture capital. VCs know that some entrepreneurs will push back after receiving a no. Following up politely is fine. However, just remember not to push so hard that you offend VCs.

The second reason to be graceful is that you need to protect your reputation as an entrepreneur. The venture community is very small. Being a jerk to one VC may affect your prospects with others. Furthermore, for most entrepreneurs, starting companies is part of their DNA; they will raise capital more than once. A smart entrepreneur has enough foresight to know that his reputation with VCs will be important to his career, not just to his current project.

One of my mentors always said that the pain in the venture process comes from the difficulty in matching investors and entrepreneurs. No two investors are the same and, as a result, most investors will not be interested in a single deal. It's not personal; it's just the way the market is designed. Assume that most VCs will not be interested, avoid getting frustrated and be polite. That will position you to come back to VCs on your next venture.

GETTING YOUR EXECUTIVE SUMMARY DISTRIBUTED TO OTHER VCS

When a VC decides not to invest in your company, they may offer to send your executive summary to another VC.

As mentioned earlier, your business must meet three high-level criteria in order to be an investment candidate:

1. A viable, high growth, scalable business
2. A good investment, capable of a large return
3. Aligned with the fund's investment criteria

If a VC does not think your venture is an attractive business, he will not distribute your business plan. He won't want to waste the time of other VCs. Similarly, if the investment return is not aligned with the requirements of other investors a VC may not circulate the opportunity. It's worth noting that investors have different return requirements and therefore if your idea is not a fit for one VC, it does not mean that another investor couldn't be interested.

If the only issue is a misalignment with the VC's thesis, they are more likely to offer to share your executive summary than if it doesn't meet either of the other two criteria. However, this is only the case if they know a VC that they think may be interested. The probability of one VC knowing potentially interested investors is typically higher if your business plan is more closely aligned to his investment thesis. VCs tend to know the other folks in their space. For example, as an IT guy it's less likely that I would be able to help a real estate startup than I would be able to help an IT venture.

The bottom line: VCs are most likely to pass along executive summaries to other VCs when the business plan is both very strong and very relevant to that VCs investment strategy.

WHY A VC MIGHT NOT SHARE YOUR EXECUTIVE SUMMARY WITH OTHER VCS

As I described, there are some scenarios in which VCs will be more comfortable sharing your executive summary with other VCs (after they have decided that they are not interested). However, even if a VC knows someone else who might be interested in your company, they won't always offer to share your executive summary. There are a few potential reasons for this:

1. They want to keep an eye on your progress and are not ready to completely pass yet.
2. They are too busy to manage that email exchange.
3. There are other politics taking place, such as the other investor looking at a syndication opportunity with your VC – your VC may not want to distract the other investor.

If the VC doesn't offer to connect you, you can ask if they know anyone who might be interested. However, if you ask and they say no, don't push them any further. Just be gracious and move on.

SHARING YOUR EXECUTIVE SUMMARY WITH ANONYMOUS VCS

A VC will often ask for your permission before sending your executive summary to one or more investors. Feel free to say no if you feel compelled. However, you should consider saying yes, as a referral from another VC is usually well received.

When giving permission to forward his executive summary, it's common for an entrepreneur to ask for the names of the other investors or to be copied on the email. However, some VCs may tell you that they prefer to keep their contacts anonymous. Typically, they do this to avoid creating work for the other investors; engaging in a chain of emails with entrepreneurs can take significant time. As a result, keeping other investors anonymous is often considered etiquette in the VC community, as it helps VCs work together without creating additional work for one another.

If you find yourself in this situation and it makes you uncomfortable, feel free to pass on the offer – your VC contact won't be offended.

THE DUE DILIGENCE PHASE

Diligencing You

THE DUE DILIGENCE PROCESS

When VCs decides they are interested, they will begin the due diligence phase. This is an important step towards netting an investment. The due diligence process is what a VC conducts to determine if he would like to invest in your company. It centers around the belief that it is more effective to assess granular aspects of a business than a business as a whole.

To illustrate this, imagine that you are an automotive mechanic. One day a car owner drives up and asks you to appraise the general condition of his car so that he can sell it. While seeing the shiny new paint job and hearing about the make of the vehicle, mileage and performance to date will be helpful, it is simply not enough information for you to guarantee that the car will perform well in the future. In order to make that assessment, you will need to evaluate all of the aspects of the car individually. You will check the breaks, test the engine and look at the tires. And then, if each of the car's key parts and processes seem to be in good shape, you can conclude that the car as a whole is likely to perform well going forward. If all the things that make up the car are in excellent condition, you can more reliably conclude that the car as a whole is in excellent condition.

This same logic applies to conducting due diligence on companies. Investors who simply look at the type of company, how long it has been around and how it has performed to date will typically not make as reliable judgments about the future viability of the company as an investor who takes a look at all of the individual aspects of a business that are required to create future value. The process of conducting due diligence forces investors to carefully check the competency of the management, test the strength of customer demand and look at future competitive dynamics. If all of the parts of the company are well oiled, it is safer to conclude that the company is ready to go the distance.

WHY VCS CONDUCT DUE DILIGENCE

The phrase "you don't know what you don't know" is the underlying rationale for the due diligence process. VCs are conducting due diligence on your company because they think some key assumptions are likely to be true. For example, they may be assuming that your market is rapidly growing or that customer will want to use your service. However, those assumptions can be wrong and VCs don't want to take that chance.

Nearly every company that a VC considers is operating in a different niche market with distinct competitive dynamics and market trends. It is critical to have a thorough understanding of these dynamics and trends when evaluating a company. The evolution of competitive dynamics and market trends dictate the extent to which a company will be successful in the future.

Obtaining a deep understanding of a marketplace is not easy to do. A substantial understanding of the marketplace can be obtained by reviewing market research, reading articles and evaluating the key competitors. But, in order to understand the nuances, investors needs to speak with key market participants, such as customers, suppliers and when possible, competitors.

It's worth noting that the VC can discover "deal killer" findings at any point in the due diligence process. Its not uncommon for the process to be nearly complete when new information is obtained that makes an investment impractical.

You must understand how important the due diligence process is to a VC so you will be patient with them and do your best to facilitate the process.

DON'T SAVE SURPRISES FOR AFTER INVESTORS COMMIT

Investors work hard to diligence investment candidates for two reasons – first, to understand the opportunity and second, to uncover potential challenges. The latter consideration can be difficult to do successfully if management elects to misrepresent the opportunity or is not forthcoming about aspects of their business.

Leaving surprises for investors to discover after they have invested is generally a bad decision for several reasons:

- These surprises breed ill-will between the investors and management, damaging board dynamics.
- These dynamics can leave management with less support for both their initiatives and ongoing participation in the company.

To avoid these situations, you should be sure to share any aspect of your business that you think will surprise investors. Whether you make these disclosures over the course of your meetings with investors or all at once, be sure to do so before you take an investor's money.

THE PHASES OF DUE DILIGENCE

There are typically two phases of the due diligence process.

The first phase typically begins after the VC has decided that he is interested in your company. At this stage, the VC begins to explore all of the key assumptions that must be true to make your company viable. Generally, these are assumptions about factors external to the business: customer demand, competitive landscape, regulatory trends and beyond. VCs examine these factors by diving into the many due diligence considerations. This first phase of diligence might start after the first meeting or even before. Some firms complete this phase before issuing a term sheet; others issue a term sheet earlier.

The second phase often begins after the term sheet is issued. In the second stage, VCs are conducting confirmatory due diligence with the goal of validating assertions by management. Confirmatory due diligence focuses on factors internal to the company, including management competency, legal considerations, and the quality of the technology.

TYPES OF DUE DILIGENCE MEETINGS

During the due diligence phase, there are two main types of meetings.

First, you will have meetings in which the primary objective is for you to meet other partners at the VC fund. A VC partner who is evaluating your company and continues to be interested will likely set this up after your first meeting in order to get another opinion and begin to build consensus around investing in your company.

VC funds are often comprised of professionals with a variety of backgrounds. These partners rely on each other for their diverse perspectives, as these unique viewpoints help them think through each investment opportunity more thoroughly. As a result, meeting other partners at a fund is a critical part of the process. You should do your best to present your case clearly to each VC so that you can earn the interest of as many of them as possible. At this stage, the objective of the meeting is the same as it was for your first meeting.

The second type of meeting that you will have during diligence is an exploratory meeting. In exploratory meetings a partner you have already met will try to learn more about your company. He or she will dive deeper into the revenue model, the market, your strategy, the how and anything else with which they are not yet comfortable. These meetings are a critical part of the process because they not only enable one or more partners to learn more about your company, but they also give those partners the information necessary to defend an investment when the group meets next. You are better off if a VC can answer all of his partners' questions about your company at the next partners meeting.

You should determine which type of meeting you are being invited to beforehand. Figuring this out is usually easy; all you need to do is ask who will attend and what will be covered at the next meeting.

EXPLORATORY MEETINGS: OPEN YOUR KIMONO

In exploratory meetings, where you are meeting with the same partner for the second, third or fourth time, your objective is very different than what it was in your first meeting with a partner at a fund. In your first meeting the objective is to get a VC interested enough to have you in for a second meeting. So, sharing too much information in the first meeting can be a mistake, if it distracts a VC from the big picture. This isn't the case in an exploratory meeting.

In an exploratory meeting, the VC is already interested; now they want to learn a lot more. You will be asked lots of diverse questions to understand the details of your plan. They will also ask about lots of details about the "how." Your objective in this meeting is to help them gain a deep understanding of your company. While you shouldn't ramble, at this stage in the game, you need to provide the VC with any color they request.

Most VCs who are interested in leading an investment in your company will want to understand a lot about your company before they invest. They will have second-order considerations about most facets of your company. For example, the qualifications of your management team will not likely be enough; they will probably also want to understand your relationship with your partner and what other roles you need to fill on the team. As the VC asks more, you will need to open your kimono wider.

Every team has skeletons in its closet. The VC will inevitably uncover some of these in these meetings. Understand that every startup has these, and don't panic. Just be honest, provide a candid assessment of the situation and focus on how these issues have been or will be resolved. Startups are messy – VCs expect there to be a need for some cleanup after the Series A.

When you get asked to an exploratory meeting, be prepared to share more color and more detail about your business. You don't want to be caught off guard when the VC starts diving in.

WHY YOU SHOULD FACILITATE DUE DILIGENCE

Some entrepreneurs view the due diligence process as a threat to their access to capital, and therefore do not make their best effort to facilitate the process. This is the wrong approach.

The due diligence process is an opportunity for the entrepreneur to achieve three key objectives:

1. **Increase VC interest:** Many VCs become increasingly excited about companies as they learn more. The more the VC can learn about your business during the due diligence process, the more excited they are likely to get. This excitement can be a valuable asset to you for building momentum.

2. **Demonstrate that you are a team player:** The due diligence process is the first time that you will work closely with a VC. For the VC, this is a glimpse into what the future of your relationship will be like, should they invest. As a result, this is your opportunity to demonstrate that you are a team player, someone who they will want to work with.

3. **Educate future board members:** This process will also help VCs become knowledgeable about your marketplace, making them even more valuable on your board. The knowledge that they gain from this process can be very different from the knowledge that you have. Customers, suppliers and business partners may tell VCs things that they would not tell you, giving your board a more complete perspective of your business.

These objectives are best met by proactively facilitating the process. Make the process easy for VCs and you will be best positioned to achieve all of these objectives.

DUE DILIGENCE CONSIDERATIONS

There are a number of common parts of the due diligence process. In fact, these steps are so commonplace that many firms have due diligence checklists that ensure they take all of the necessary steps in the process.

Ultimately, the due diligence considerations are typically segmented based upon each of the key strategic, operational and financial elements of a company. Each consideration is typically assessed through a combination of meeting with management, review of secondary research, and conversations with industry participants (e.g., customer, competitors, investors, experts).

Due diligence considerations:

- Business model and addressable market size
- Customer demand
- Competitive advantages
- Business development marketing plan
- Technology and product development
- Operations management and human resources
- Financial
- Legal

These considerations are addressed through a number of common activities:

- Customer calls
- Expert calls
- Partner calls
- Addressable market sizing
- Model review
- Competitive landscape assessment
- Management reference calls

CUSTOMER REFERENCE CALLS

When a VC conducts due diligence, he typically wants to conduct calls with current or future customers in order to understand the customers' perspectives on your business. These calls are a critical part of the due diligence process, as VCs often won't know your customers' perspectives about your service as well as you do. As a result, investors will have to validate that customers actually have the perspective that you have described. For example, a VC will want to hear several customers confirm that they:

- View the problem that you are solving a significant pain point,
- Believe that your service will be the best solution,
- Are willing to pay the prices you included in your model, and
- Intend to use your service as often as you have projected.

VCs typically only call "warm" contacts. By "warm," I mean contacts that the VC either has a relationship with already or has been introduced to by the entrepreneur or a third party. VCs generally avoid "cold" calls because it often takes a lot of time to find people who are willing to speak with someone they don't know. Since VCs are generally very busy, they want to use this time in the most efficient way possible.

More often than not, the entrepreneur will set up calls with customers for the VC. This process is generally pretty straightforward. The entrepreneur calls a customer, explains that they are being evaluated by a potential investor, and asks if the customer would mind speaking to the VC about their service. However, it is probably wise for entrepreneurs to position the call with the VC casually, as either relatively low importance to the continued operation of the company or one of many investors being engaged. In so doing, if the VC decides not to invest, customers don't get nervous about the viability of the venture.

You should also keep in mind that it could annoy your customers if they have to do diligence calls with a slew of VCs. You should only permit the VCs with the highest likelihood of investing to make these calls.

Entrepreneurs who have businesses in stealth mode (meaning that they are still keeping their business idea a secret) may find this process of having a third party call their customers a bit unnerving. They might fear that this conversation could expose their idea. While it is worth noting that this is rarely a concern of entrepreneurs who are engaging VCs because their businesses are already or soon-to-be unveiled, there is a way to mitigate this risk while still enabling the VC to hear the customer viewpoint. All you have to do is simply ask the VC to keep the concept a secret. If you do this, good VCs will ask questions in a manner that conceals your business strategy.

Other entrepreneurs may find this process to be a valuable way to enhance their business. If the VC happens to know a potential customer that you were not in contact with they may call on that person and ask questions that ultimately generate interest in your service.

Ultimately, most VCs will need to make customer calls in order to invest, or at least depend on the diligence collected by other VCs during similar calls. If you want to raise venture capital, be prepared to set up customer calls.

FILLING INFORMATION GAPS: EXPERTS

While most VCs know a lot about running businesses and investing, it is rare that a VC will know more about a specific business than the entrepreneur who is launching a company. The entrepreneur needs to have a unique degree of expertise and knowledge about his target market in order to devise a viable disruptive strategy. As a result, VCs typically have less information than the entrepreneur about the prospects of company that they are investing in. To mitigate some of this information asymmetry, VCs lean on experts.

Expert is a loosely defined term here. It includes anyone who knows a significant amount about at least one aspect of the market in question. An expert might be an analyst who spends every waking hour thinking about this market or it might be a person who knows a lot about one aspect of this deal, such as the technology, customers, a government regulatory body or competitors.

VCs contact these experts because they often provide the quickest way to learn a lot about an industry, enabling the VC to get another perspective about considerations that present concerns. In a one-hour call, an expert can give a VC the scoop, laying out the industry dynamics and highlighting the key issues that they should be thinking about.

Furthermore, these experts can validate key assumptions. If the viability of an entrepreneur's whole business hinges on a key factor, such as incumbents not entering the market or customers being really frustrated by the current value proposition offered in the industry, an expert can provide some validation.

Entrepreneurs should be aware that VCs are going to contact experts when they conduct due diligence. It is worth noting that they can do this without disclosing your business idea; these conversations are often one-way. Experts understand that the VC can't disclose key information and usually don't mind sharing their wisdom.

Entrepreneurs should use the knowledge that VCs will likely rely on experts to their advantage. Founders can both expedite and shape the due diligence process by identifying experts for VCs. This enables entrepreneurs to increase the likelihood that the VCs are hearing perspectives that support their vision and it cuts out the time that VCs spend in trying to find and connect with thought leaders.

MITIGATING PARTNERSHIP RISK: HEARING IT FROM THE HORSE'S MOUTH

Some businesses rely heavily on securing key partnerships. While entrepreneurs will often make compelling cases for why the prospective partner will want to get involved, there are often unforeseen reasons why the partner never inks the deal. Key decision makers may be in a political struggle, they could be considering doing the same thing internally, the fight for budget allocations may not have gone in favor of the partnering department, and the list goes on.

As a result, a VC will typically try to mitigate its exposure to the risk that the partnership will not be secured by having direct conversations with the potential partner. If they hear the partner say that the deal is going to get done, it is much easier to believe in the prospects of the startup.

If your company is currently in negotiations with the partner, you will have to weigh the pros and cons of having the VC speak with them. While the VC call may add a new dynamic to your relationship with the partner, it may also signal to the partner that your startup is close to having deep pockets supporting it, mitigating financial risks. In this case, you have to make a judgment call, which typically boils down to letting the VC speak with your potential partner or waiting to get funding after the partnership deal gets done.

If you have not yet initiated conversations with your potential partner, you can leverage the VC due diligence process to initiate those relationships. Most good VCs have a deep Rolodex and can find a way to get in touch with the person who would consider doing that deal with you. Not only can they make the introduction, but also they can give your company significant credibility when they are first introduced to the potential partner. When the potential partner receives a call from a respected VC who says, "We are looking at an interesting startup right now that could present a partnership opportunity for you. Would you mind having a conversation with them? We would love to hear your perspective on what they are doing." If a serious investor is interested in your company, the potential partner will likely give conversations with your firm more weight.

If your strategy depends on securing one or more key partnerships, be prepared to facilitate the conversations that are required to give the investor comfort. And, if you have yet to connect with the partner, you may want to leverage the due diligence process to help get the deal done.

SANITY CHECK: IS YOUR ADDRESSABLE MARKET SIZE REALISTIC?

During the diligence phase, a VC will take a deeper look at your addressable market. I first discussed addressable markets under *Preparing Your Materials* above. A significant number of entrepreneurs confuse the concept of market size and addressable market size (an addressable market is the total revenue that your company would generate if it captured every single viable revenue-generating opportunity). Even those who understand this distinction often don't calculate the right number.

Addressable market estimates are typically soft in the sense that they are a compilation of estimates. However, they are still extremely valuable for investment decision-making. If each assumption is reasonable, meaning in the range of realistic outcomes given the best available information, then the output of the exercise will usually generate an answer that is in the right order of magnitude (meaning it has the right number of digits). It is helpful to know that if the company captured every revenue-generating opportunity it could realize revenue in the millions, tens of millions, hundreds of millions, billions or more.

Where many entrepreneurs go wrong when they are calculating their addressable market is that they don't get the assumptions right. There are two types of mistakes that are most common:

- **Assumptions are not sufficiently refined:** Entrepreneurs often exclude some of the logic that goes into this analysis, which more often than not shrinks the output of this calculation. For example, an e-tailer selling T-ball bats isn't going to sell bats to every person in the US. Not everyone plays T-ball. So, when this estimate is being created the US population needs to be refined by another factor, the percentage of people who play T-ball.
- **Assumptions are simply over-estimated:** Entrepreneurs sometimes inflate inputs into the addressable market calculation. Demographic segments are often enlarged and CPM rates overstated. If you feel compelled to demonstrate the best-case scenario, it's always best to create a low and a high case, which will demonstrate the range of possible outcomes. This approach will highlight upside while letting investors know that you are aware of business realities.

There are a couple of key reasons to be careful not to make these mistakes. First, good VCs will catch the errors, and second, when they catch the errors it will raise questions about management competency.

In addition to the problems created when entrepreneurs overestimate the size of their addressable market, I want to touch on the problems created by underestimating the opportunity.

It's rare that addressable markets are underestimated by entrepreneurs. However, it does happen, especially when the entrepreneur is very analytical and focused on not overselling.

Underestimating the opportunity creates two key challenges for the entrepreneur:

- First, VCs may take the number as a given and miss the real opportunity.
- Second, it raises questions about the entrepreneur's faith in the larger prospects of the company.

An additional challenge is that it highlights that the CEO may not be a natural salesperson. While that's not inherently an issue, it can become one if the CEO is not aware of this weakness. This could lead to a situation where the CEO positions the company's future to be dependent upon their sales ability, rather than finding another person to join the team who can lead the sales effort.

Like most things in life, moderation is the key. Both overestimating and underestimating can be detrimental.

Don't force your addressable market size fit into a VC's thesis by artificially manipulating the market numbers. You are better off trying to raise money from other parties who will be interested in your company (such as angels). Trying to force a square peg in a round hole can hurt your credibility.

WHY VCS WANT TO REVIEW YOUR MODEL

VCs can check a few different aspects of your business by reviewing your model.

First and foremost, they can assess your understanding of your business model (how you generate revenue). The logic in the math should demonstrate the drivers of value for the business. If the model reflects an understanding of these relationships, the VCs can often assume that it is focusing on their right objectives.

Second, the model should illustrate the operating plan for the company. Headcounts and expenses should be clear. For example, after a quick look the VC should be able to find the number of salespeople over time and office space expenses. One of the most important aspects of these models is that they can demonstrate your team's ability to think through the operational requirements of managing this business. It should answer some of the "how" questions, such as, "How many salespeople will it take to generate $1 million of revenue?"

Third, the model should help VCs understand some of the quantitative relationships in the business. For example, they can evaluate the types of margins that the company generates and the viability of the marketing strategy (making sure that the cost of customer acquisition is aligned with the life-time value of each customer).

This is a very important part of the due diligence process. It is critical that the model is easy to navigate and sufficiently granular to demonstrate key relationships and assumptions.

COMPETITIVE POSITIONING: MAKING THE VC COMFORTABLE

Barring unique regulatory or patent protection, no company has a perfectly defensible business model. This holds true for companies of all sizes; even a significant portion of the Fortune 500 has turned over during the past century.

However, this doesn't mean that believing in the competitive positioning of a company in not important to investors. Investors need to believe that the company is positioned to win in its marketplace. While the competitive assessment that you provide to investors in your business plan will certainly be very helpful, it is typically not enough to make the investor comfortable.

As a result, investors typically like to do a little research of their own in order to both learn more about potential competitors and your company's potential barriers. Potential competitors are identified in a few ways. At the simplest level, VCs will scour the web to see which companies are already in the space and which companies are positioned to become competitors in the future. VCs will also look to experts (e.g., CEOs of portfolio companies in adjacent markets) to fill some of these gaps.

In order to assess your company's barriers, VCs will spend time thinking strategically about the means of competition in the market. If success is solely based upon your team's ability to operate more efficiently than your competitors, VCs will need to know who is managing your competitors. If barriers are created through scale, then the VC will spend a lot of time thinking about whether or not your company is positioned to grow the fastest. They will ask questions such as: Do you have the best model? The greatest access to customers and partners? The most desirable product?

The best thing that an entrepreneur can do to help VCs get comfortable with the competitive landscape is to 1) identify competitors and 2) make the case for why your company is positioned to win.

1. **Identify competitors:** It is always disconcerting to VCs when they discover a new competitor late in the process. It makes the VC feel that

either the entrepreneur wasn't forth coming about competitive risks, raising questions about the compatibility of management, or the entrepreneur doesn't know their market very well.

2. **Make your case:** When a VC starts doing research on the other companies, they are going to hear lots of different arguments about the competitive viability of each company. If they are not hearing your perspective, they may only hear the other side of the story. If this happens, they may not be fully aware about your company's prospects. It is the entrepreneur's role to ensure that the VC understands his view of the opportunity.

MANAGEMENT REFERENCES: THE ETHICS TEST

In order to invest, VCs must trust that the entrepreneurs they are backing have the capacity to execute. VCs assess management's ability in a few ways.

The ability to think strategically can be demonstrated through the quality of your business idea and plan. Your understanding of operations can be illustrated by answering the "how" and sharing your model. Finally, your compatibility is assessed through all of your interactions with the VC. However, knowing that you get along, are capable of executing and really understand your business is not enough. VCs also need to know that you are ethical.

While there are plenty of laws protecting investors from fraudulent activity, unethical entrepreneurs can create lots of problems for VCs. First and foremost, there are always lots of grey ethical zones, where entrepreneurs can choose to create problems for other shareholders without incurring clear legal liability. Second, even if a legal boundary is crossed, the process of taking action is expensive, time consuming and a distraction from other portfolio companies. As a result, it is in the best interest of VCs to avoid making investments in people who are not really team players.

In order to mitigate the chances of investing in unethical management teams, VCs speak to management's references. References are typically asked about their experience working with the entrepreneurs and through their answers, VCs draw conclusions about management's moral compass.

There are two elements to this test. The first is simply the entrepreneur's ability to generate a list of people that would be willing to speak on their behalf. If an entrepreneur hasn't impressed anyone with work ethic and intellect enough to merit a reference, then the investor has reason to be concerned.

Second, these references can shed light on the entrepreneur's ethics. While these references can serve to validate more than management's moral compass, reaffirmation of the competency of an individual is not typically the primary objective of the call. There is good reason for this.

First, by the time references are being called, VCs have already decided that the individual is probably talented. This doesn't mean that references may highlight significant concerns about management's ability to execute; it's just that it doesn't happen often.

Second, management typically provides the VC with the list of references, ensuring that the VC speaks to people whom they believe will say favorable things about their work. However, an old boss who thought the entrepreneur's work was top-notch may harbor concerns about their ability to be a team player or make ethical decisions. Entrepreneurs are less likely to be aware of these perceptions because they are typically less integrated in standard feedback mechanism. You can get a promotion or a raise even if your manager wouldn't trust you to watch their children. This dynamic makes these reference calls more meaningful for testing ethical considerations.

Entrepreneurs and key managers who are progressing through the due diligence process should be prepared to share a list of personal references with investors. Ideally there should be five to 10 names on the list to demonstrate that the individual has made a positive impact on a number of people. The list should include for each reference:

- Description of the reference's relationship to the entrepreneur
- Phone number
- Email address
- Time zone (if relevant)

MANAGE VC EXPECTATIONS ABOUT OPERATING PERFORMANCE

It's not uncommon for an entrepreneur to talk up a big customer sale or partnership deal that is in process when trying to get a VC interested. However, if the deal falls through, presenting a potential milestone to a VC as validation of your company can come back to hurt you. These blessings can turn into curses.

Therefore, entrepreneurs should be careful to manage VC expectations during the due diligence phase. It's wise to emphasize the risk associated with key deals with customers and partners. However, while presenting these risks, entrepreneurs should still position the fact that customers and partners are engaging in these conversations as a good sign that the market is interested in your business. This way, if the deal falls through you can still emphasize the potential to get future deals done, moving the VCs focus away from the loss of this deal.

For example, you wouldn't want to say, "This company is a home run, we're about to lock up a deal with a Fortune 500 company." Rather, I would suggest that you position it as "We're already starting to speak with Fortune 500 companies. Those deals are never a certainty, but the very fact that we're getting traction demonstrates the market's interest in what we're doing." Until of course, you sign a deal, in which case you should shout the fact from the investors' rooftops.

If you carefully manage expectations about your short-term operating performance, you will reduce the number of things that can derail a VC's interest.

EVOLVE

VCs use the due diligence process for more than collecting information and learning about your company. They want to back entrepreneurs who can solve problems by evolving when necessary. Fortunately for VCs, there is an easy way for them to test this. Nobody has exactly the right plan from the beginning and startups face model-shaping challenges all the time. As a result, VCs often have the chance to watch an entrepreneur respond to issues during the diligence period. How entrepreneurs handle these issues will help VCs decide whether they believe the management team is prepared to take the company through the startup phase (if not further).

Furthermore, VCs often enter the due diligence phase with awareness of an issue that management has yet to address. In these situations, VCs take the opportunity to make suggestions and watch how entrepreneurs respond to feedback. Doing so provides a great test of how the entrepreneur will work with VCs after the investment. If you are a team player who takes feedback to heart, you will do well.

Being aware of this dynamic during the due diligence phase can help you prove to VCs that you are going to be a compatible partner in the future.

DO THE FOUNDER'S PERSONAL FINANCES MATTER?

I have been asked if VCs consider an entrepreneur's personal credit history and finances when making an investment decision. Unless an entrepreneur's credit history evinces an inability to manage a budget, the personal wealth of the entrepreneur is a more relevant consideration.

VCs want to back entrepreneurs who are highly driven. However, entrepreneurs are motivated by different things. While some are driven by money, others are driven by passion for creation, a desire for prestige or any number of other motivations.

The situation in which I have seen the personal wealth of an entrepreneur considered in the investment process was when the entrepreneur is already wealthy. I have found that wealthy entrepreneurs can be viewed as more risky given the perception that they have less to lose. This also raises questions about how hard the entrepreneur will work on the startup – one consideration of many in an investment decision. It's worth noting that this particular concern can be mitigated by the entrepreneur having sufficient skin in the game (his or her own money invested in the company).

Dilgencing the VC

DOING DUE DILIGENCE ON THE VC

Managing a startup is a tremendous undertaking in itself. Managing a startup, while raising money, is a Herculean task. By the time that the due diligence is complete, an entrepreneur is usually exhausted and eager to be done with the fundraising process. However, this is a key time for entrepreneurs to ensure that they are working with the right partner.

The importance of hiring the right people is a principle that holds true for your investors too. Investors offer more than money, they offer operating assets (e.g., contacts and ideas) and they also become affiliated with your company in the minds of outsiders. Having the right investors can really help you and having the wrong ones can hurt you.

Bad investors can be too controlling, create unnecessary headaches and make decisions solely for their personal short-term financial gain; a bad investor takes more than they give. Furthermore, a bad investor can deter good investors from getting involved in the future.

As a result, in order to make sure that the investors can truly be a value add, both with internal operations and external perceptions, you will need to conduct due diligence on VCs. The best way to do this is to ask the VC for references who can vouch for the VC. Typically, these come in the form of entrepreneurs that the VC has backed in the past.

It's important to note that few entrepreneurs conduct due diligence on VCs. This is probably because they don't have the time, don't have more than one potential investor and have already asked their trusted advisers about the VC in question. As a result, VCs are not entirely accustomed to facilitating this type of due diligence, creating a need for you to broach this topic somewhat carefully as you might catch them off guard. Ultimately, you should use your best interpersonal skills to find a friendly way to ask for some references.

These references can prove to be valuable even if the VC is your only potential investor and you intend to take their money regardless of the feedback you hear. References can help shed light onto the VC's strengths/weaknesses and overall style. This can help prepare you to interact with them effectively when they join your board.

MAKE SURE YOUR VC ISN'T A JERK

I once heard another VC offer simple advice that entrepreneurs should take to heart: "Make sure your VC isn't a jerk."

It's a simple bit of advice and likely obvious to many. It does, however, deserve more weight in the decision-making process than it is given by most entrepreneurs. Unfortunately, entrepreneurs don't always have many options when it comes to capital sources, making it difficult to be picky about whom they partner with. When there are options, many entrepreneurs will prioritize getting the best deal over taking money from investors who will behave like partners. That's a mistake.

Bad partners can cause lots of problems for your company, especially when times get tough. For example, these types of investors may not be willing to provide your company with working capital to tide you over before the next round (when it would be appropriate to do so). Or, they might be the naysayers who make many straightforward operational and financial decisions difficult to pass through the board. The list of potential challenges that a bad partner can create is long.

My intention here isn't to suggest that you won't face conflict and disagreement with good partners. The difference is that good partners will always be acting in good faith to make reasonable decisions. The bad partners are those who don't act in good faith.

The inherent challenge is that when you take money from a bad VC, it feels as though your problems have ended. You're now capitalized – the anxiety is gone – you're now safe for a while. In reality, however, the addition of a bad VC to your capital table may only be the beginning of your problems.

There are good VCs in the marketplace. If you can, take their money.

HOW TO IDENTIFY "JERK" VCS

There are ways for entrepreneurs to identify the good partners by doing a little homework.

The first way to determine if a VC will make a good partner is by doing a gut check. Did the VC seem like someone you can trust? Some questions to ask yourself: 1) Were they really sales-y or genuine? 2) Did they discuss the business with you the way a partner would, or did they seem to have a different agenda?

You might ask the VC some questions in the meeting to refine your gut check. Remember, you're interviewing them too.

It's also worthwhile to have the other members of your team do a gut check on the investors when the VC meets the team. Your partners should all give their input on the VC and you might want to also get the read of your head of sales, as the sales team often has a more acute ability to read people.

I'm using the word "references" broadly here.

Ask around the local community to get a sense for the word on the street about the investor. As part of this effort, you should check out some of the investor review websites such as thefunded.com or otherwise. Be aware, however, that some of the comments on there are likely to be furnished by disgruntled entrepreneurs. VCs are, after all, set up to be bad guys, and (as customer service studies tell us) angry customers are more likely to complain than satisfied ones. If most of the comments are positive, you're probably engaging a reasonable partner.

Towards the end of the investment process, you should also conduct reverse due diligence on the VC and speak to CEOs of their portfolio companies to get a sense of how helpful they have been.

DOING THE DEAL

How Deals Get Done

TIMING OF VC INVESTMENTS

VCs have conflicting incentives when it comes to how long they should wait before formally offering you a term sheet.

First, by extending the due diligence period, VCs can learn more about your business plan, how your management team operates and how the market is evolving. Put another way, the longer they wait, the more likely they are to invest in a winner because as more time passes some risks can be mitigated or disappear altogether. For example, if a VC can invest after the product is launched, they may be able to invest knowing how consumers respond to the product, limiting some of the adoption risk.

However, VCs also have an incentive to act quickly. In a competitive venture market, being the first to put a term sheet down can be an advantage. The main advantage of being first is that a VC may make the term sheet an "exploding offer" (meaning it expires within a defined time frame), forcing the entrepreneur to accept the offer before other firms can offer a term sheet. Furthermore, being first can create goodwill with entrepreneurs as it demonstrates seriousness and the ability to act.

Ultimately, VCs time their diligence process based on their needs. If they need to learn more before getting to "yes," then they'll take more time. If they are ready to invest and worried about other VCs taking the deal, they'll act more quickly.

THE OBJECTIVES OF THE ALL-PARTNER MEETING

Some of the common partnership structures require each entrepreneur to make a presentation to the entire partnership before the VC partnership makes a final decision to invest.

There are four objectives for this meeting:

1. Familiarize all of the partners with your business,
2. Address concerns,
3. Demonstrate the competency of your team, and
4. Keep the momentum going and get the team to "yes."

The best way to prepare is to ask your primary contact at the firm about the level of knowledge about your company within the partnership and the key concerns. This will enable you to gauge how detailed to be and which issues you need to address.

However, in the absence of that guidance, my next few sections will provide some generic advice on how to achieve these goals.

Inform

When you are at the all-partner meeting, you should assume that some of the partners know nothing about your company. It's likely that most of the partners will have heard at least a little about your company before the meeting. However, there will probably be a few that have your executive summary sitting in a pile on their desk or in an unread email in their inbox. As a result, your presentation should be sure to cover most of the high level aspects of your business. I recommend having an investment overview slide.

Alleviate Concerns

During the presentation, be prepared to change course. If a partner asks a question, you need to stop your pitch and address that issue on the spot. At this stage in the process, you can't let major concerns linger. When you hear issues, you should try to put them to rest ASAP, as any outstanding concerns that are not addressed may reverberate in the ensuing meetings that the partners have. If you put these fires out early you can increase your odds of getting approved.

Demonstrate Competency

The third objective is demonstrating competency. The best way to do this is to simply have a clear presentation and provide clear answers to questions.

If you have gotten to this point in the process, the firm is seriously considering making an investment. However, deals die in all stages of the process. Make sure to spend the time preparing for this presentation.

Close the Deal

While you are bringing the new partners up to speed, putting out fires, and demonstrating competency, you also need to close the deal. Closing the deal at this stage means both creating excitement and a sense of urgency.

To create excitement you need to help the people in the room see your vision. In my opinion the difference between getting other people to see your vision and not often comes down to clearly stating implicit conclusions. For example, saying "people will use this product" isn't enough. Complete the logic so that nobody misses the point: "People will use this product and as a result we are positioned to generate hundreds of millions of dollars each year." The value in this technique is several-fold:

1. It ensures that everyone in the room draws the same conclusions that you are (or at least understands the conclusions that you are making),
2. It increases the odds that people who are still focused on processing something you said a few minutes ago will hear the big picture point,
3. People have an easier time understanding the causality inherent in a well-delineated narrative.

While you will have to work to create excitement throughout the entire presentation, developing a sense of urgency only takes a few subtle comments. The best way to do this is to indicate that real time constraints exist, such as alternative exploding term sheets or contingent partnership deals. However, in the absence of hard deadlines, you can still create urgency with more subtle comments such as, "We're moving forward with the company very rapidly and would like you to be involved." This delicately implies that the VCs could be left behind.

SIGNS YOU'RE CLOSE TO A TERM SHEET

Entrepreneurs in the due diligence phase are often eager to know when they will receive a term sheet. Unfortunately, the due diligence process varies by venture firm, making the timing a bit variable. However, there are some common signs that the term sheet is coming soon.

First and foremost, the best way to know that a term sheet is coming is when your contact at the venture fund tells you. Good VCs are sensitive to your situation as an entrepreneur and will provide you with some transparency as to where you are in the process, openly communicating the next steps for due diligence and the likely timing. However, communication is stylistic and not all VCs will be forthcoming. In these situations, it's okay to ask VCs about their process and expected timing.

In the event that the VC does not communicate about the process, there are a few other common signs that the due diligence process is coming to a close:

- You meet all of the other partners at one meeting. While one partner will often spearhead due diligence on your company, most VC firms require some level of partnership approval for each investment. As a result, when the due diligence process is coming to a close and the lead partner is close to wanting to make an investment, they will often invite you in to meet with the entire partnership to get a sense of you and your company. This will enable them to vote on whether or not to invest. Ultimately, when you are invited to meet the partnership, the term sheet is probably not far away.

- VCs start talking terms. Also, when VCs start talking about specific terms, including your current capitalization, shareholder expectations and other drivers that factor into the development of the term sheet, they are likely starting to develop a proposed term sheet and post-money cap table. Creating a term sheet and cap table is often one of the last steps before creating a term sheet and is usually a good sign that an offer will be made soon.

Note that being close to receiving a term sheet doesn't mean that you will get one. VCs can discover deal-killing information at any point before the investment is made. While these signs should give you reason to be optimistic about receiving a term sheet, it's wise to remain cautiously optimistic.

WHEN VCS ISSUE TERM SHEETS

VC term sheets provide the investors with a fixed amount of time to conduct additional due diligence on the company before the deal closes. In this due diligence window, the VC can opt to terminate the deal.

VCs vary in the way in which they use this diligence period – some use this period for the bulk of their diligence, others only use it for the final diligence considerations. As a result, there are two points in the investment process when VCs typically issue term sheets: before due diligence or before confirmatory due diligence.

VC funds that issue term sheets before the due diligence process typically do a deep dive into their external diligence on the company after the term sheet is issued. The external research that I refer to here includes market evaluation, a review of the competitive landscape, customer calls and a testing of other unique considerations (e.g., regulatory reform).

However, VCs who issue term sheets after they complete (or nearly complete) their external due diligence still conduct confirmatory due diligence after the term sheet is issued. Confirmatory due diligence might include management reference calls and a review of the company's actual financials, patents and contracts. Confirmatory due diligence is, by and large, a review of the claims management made which are likely to be less subjective in nature.

While exceptions exist, most funds are consistent about issuing their term sheets at the same point in the process. Each fund either issues term sheets before any due diligence or after the external due diligence but before the confirmatory due diligence.

SHARING YOUR CAP TABLE

A "cap table," or capitalization table, details the equity ownership and debt obligations of the company. When a VC gives you a term sheet, it will include a cap table that reflects the post-investment ownership levels of key parties.

In order to prepare the term sheet, you will need to provide the VC with your pre-investment (pre-money) cap table. This will enable them to make a proposal that balances all of the key considerations: their ownership and the ownership of the entrepreneurs.

When you send the VC a cap table, it's best not to include a target post-investment (post-money) cap table. Here are a few reasons not to include a post-money cap table:

- It's a bad way to start the negotiation, since it appears to be a passive aggressive mechanism for proposing the valuation.
- You may propose a lower valuation than a VC intended to offer.
- It makes you look uninformed about the fundraising process, since it is commonplace for VCs to make the first term sheet offer.

The only exception is that you may want to give guidance regarding the size of the option pool you believe should be in place post-financing. The VC will expect you to have an informed opinion on this subject given your assessment of the hiring and related equity compensation needs of the company.

With this one exception, though, the best strategy here is to provide a simple and clear cap table.

WHAT IT MEANS TO RECEIVE A TERM SHEET

As stated above, VCs typically issue term sheets either before due diligence or after the majority of their external due diligence, but before confirmatory due diligence.

Term sheets issued earlier in the investment process (before due diligence) typically carry with them less of a commitment from the VC to invest. This shouldn't be too much of a surprise, since there is more due diligence left to do that may unveil information that will change a VC's interest in the company.

In my experience, the best early-stage VCs do much of their diligence before issuing a term sheet. At the time when these VCs issue a term sheet, they will typically have decided that they like your market, your model, your team and the general prospects of your startup. For the best early stage funds, the issuance of a term sheet is a strong statement of interest, and is nearly a commitment to invest.

In fact, I have heard that VCs who issue term sheets later in the process cite statistics about how infrequently they have walked away from an investment after issuing a term sheet (some claim they never have), highlighting the level of commitment a term sheet can signify.

Investment intentions can vary when a VC issues a term sheet. It's important to ask the VC what type of commitment issuing a term sheet is to them.

TERM SHEETS: EXPLODING OFFERS

One of my mentors once said, VCs love to be the first to be second. They don't want to be the first to issue a term sheet, but will issue one quickly once someone else has.

As a result, VCs often make their term sheets exploding offers – they expire within a defined timeframe. This enables them to reduce the odds that other VCs will be able to make competitive bids to invest in the startup before the entrepreneur has to make a decision.

If you like the VC you're working with and the terms are fair, this isn't an issue. However, this dynamic is something that you should be aware of, as you will need to be prepared to quickly review the terms of the term sheet.

The good news is that term sheets typically aren't issued out of the blue – if you watch for the signs that you are close to receiving a term sheet, you can be prepared to respond to exploding offers.

THE NO SHOP CLAUSE

When a VC issues a term sheet, it typically includes a no shop clause, which prohibits the entrepreneur from speaking to other investors while the VC completes his due diligence.

Therefore, it's very important that an entrepreneur asks the VC what his intentions are when he issues the term sheet. Many early stage VCs view the issuance of a term sheet as a statement of an intention to invest, barring unexpected findings during due diligence.

However, for entrepreneurs who engage in no shop clauses with VCs who don't view the issuance of a term sheet as an indication of a serious intention to invest, entering into a no shop clause can significantly delay the fundraising process. If the VC elects not to invest after requiring you to cease discussions with other investors, you may lose the interest of other potential investors and could waste a lot of time.

SAVE A SLIVER OF YOUR ROUND

If your raise goes really well, you'll be oversubscribed. Despite the demand to participate in your round, if your investors are supportive, you might want to hold some of the round for strategic investors in the future.

It's not uncommon to structure investment documents to permit future closings – meaning investors can participate in your round under the same terms as your current investors. Typically this is done to enable investors who commit now to fund the investment later. If a VC has yet to close a new fund or if someone is out of town, the future closing will enable them to participate.

While it's atypical to keep part of the round open without a predetermined investor in mind, you can do it. For example, you could hold $25,000 - $50,000 of your round open for a future closing, hoping you'll find a particularly value-add investor over the course of the coming months. Maybe a large customer or a well-known VC or a person who knows everyone in your target industry would like to invest.

Typically the period in which future closes can be conducted is predefined – often allowing them to take place in up to three to six months after the initial close. If you'll want the additional capital in the company, you may want to make sure one of your existing buyers will fill the remaining investment if you don't find another suitor along the way.

STRUCTURING YOUR CLOSE

Whether bringing capital into a debt or equity round, you can technically have all of your investors invest in one closing (at the same time) or over numerous closings (at different times). When investors invest at different times, it's called a rolling close.

What's attractive about a rolling close is that it enables the company to both 1) take in money as soon as their first investor is ready and 2) to accommodate the timing constraints faced by other investors. Exogenous factors can prevent an investor from being ready to fund – capital can get locked up, people travel, etc., which could prevent someone from participating in your round if you have a rigid single closing.

So why not always do a rolling close? They are, with few exceptions, more advantageous to entrepreneurs. The answer: they can scare some investors. In a rolling close investors typically sign their contracts when they are about to fund the company; investors will often officially sign their contracts at different times. Since investors are typically not obligated to invest until they have signed on the dotted line, early investors can get anxious about being the only players in the syndicate.

Here's what they're worried about: If one minority investor puts some capital into the company and everyone else chickens out, the early investors will be exposed to financing risk. In this scenario, financing risk is the risk that the company runs out of cash, leaving them with the tough choice of 1) giving the company more money than originally intended in order to protect their initial investment or 2) watching their initial investment evaporate. Of course, this is only a problem if the rest of the investors don't materialize, but it is a risk.

To combat this concern, most convertible notes compensate investors with a discount (the ability to get more shares for the same investment) that increases until the round is closed.

There are no black or white rules for how to handle this – just a lot of gray. At the end of the day, putting a rolling close in place is more convenient, but your ability to enforce it will be a function of investor sophistication and interest.

11

DEAL TERMS: RIGHTS TO FUTURE CASH

Valuation

VENTURE VALUATION OVERVIEW

There are many elements associated with a venture investment. However, the most prominent consideration is valuation. At the highest level, there are three components in this calculation: pre-money valuation, new equity, and post-money valuation.

The pre-money valuation refers to the value of the company before taking new money (the investment) from the VC. At its essence, this metric reflects the standalone value of the company at the time of investment.

New equity is all of the capital that converts to equity during the investment round. This includes new capital from investors (VCs, angels or otherwise) and all debt that converts to equity in this round.

Figuring out the appropriate amount of new capital to raise is complicated, as both the entrepreneurs and investors have conflicting incentives; each are incented to both raise more and less. Finding the right amount usually results from a thoughtful and well-intentioned dialog between the two parties.

The post-money valuation is the value of the company after the investment has been made. This value is equal to the sum of the pre-money valuation and the amount of new equity. The intuition behind this is pretty simple. The company didn't lose any value during the transaction, so the standalone (pre-money) value of the company remains the same. And a dollar is worth a dollar whether it's in the pocket of a VC or in the coffers of a startup. As a result, the value of the company post-investment (post-money) is the pre-money plus new equity.

PRE-MONEY DOES NOT EQUAL THE LAST ROUND'S POST-MONEY

It is important to note that a company's pre-money valuation is not the same as the post-money valuation of the prior investment round. The rationale behind this is pretty simple – companies typically increase in value over time as they continue to improve their operations and acquire more revenue. Therefore, as the underlying value of the company increases, so does the valuation of the company when it's raising additional capital.

PRE-MONEY VALUATION IS NET OF DEBT

Since the pre-money valuation reflects the valuation of the company as a standalone entity, this value is reflective of all the value-creating and detracting factors. The pre-money value inherently represents the underlying value of the company (products, customer relationships, brand, etc) minus the value of outstanding obligations, such as debt. As a result, the pre-money valuation is net of debt.

However, it's worth noting that debt that is set to convert to equity during the investment round will not be treated as debt and subtracted from the pre-money valuation. Rather, since the debt will convert to equity it is treated as an equity investment, as it will impact the capital table going forward.

THE ARCANE METHOD OF VALUING EARLY-STAGE COMPANIES

Early-stage investment firms likely vary in the process that they use to determine valuations for Seed and Series A investments. Companies at this stage are often pre-revenue (or even pre-product). That said, the common thread between the various approaches to valuing early-stage companies is that ultimately they all are as much art as science. Judgment and experience are key inputs into the process; a mathematical equation alone rarely yields the appropriate output.

Unfortunately, no single equation is designed to optimize all of the VC's key objectives. In general, VCs need to find a deal structure that balances three key considerations. The terms must be:

- More attractive than the entrepreneur's other options,
- Provide the VC with ownership sufficient to generate an acceptable risk-adjusted return, and
- Designed to provide key managers with enough equity to align incentives.

Because there isn't a single equation that solves for all three of these objectives, valuations are most often determined through a process of scenario analysis. A range of valuations and capital investments are put into a capitalization table model. The output, which illustrates the ownership of all of the involved parties after the investment, is then evaluated to determine if it achieves the three objectives stated above. If it does not, the inputs (valuation and capital invested) are adjusted until a viable scenario is identified.

As part of this math, VCs typically do an additional analysis whereby they project their expected ownership levels after future dilution to understand the likely return on investment in various exit scenarios. This analysis can help them better assess how much of the company they need to own initially in order to generate an acceptable return after dilution.

The fact that the valuation process is based on judgment does not mean that it is invalid. I would argue that all company valuations, whether the company is early or late stage, are in no small part based on judgment. Regardless of what equation or process is used, some of the inputs ultimately are dependent upon investor experience. For example, in a discounted cash flows model (an approach often used for valuing more mature companies), the process used for selecting a discount rate is often less than scientific (and arguably arbitrary). Small variances in discount rate can have a large impact on the ultimate valuation. The same holds true for the process of selecting and adjusting comparables used in both early and later stage valuation exercises. Picking one comparable company over another or selecting one arbitrary adjustment over another can substantially impact the valuation.

Regardless of the methodology used to arrive at a valuation, investor willingness to pay determines the range of acceptable outcomes. Simply put, investors won't pay more than their perceived value of the company.

HOW VCS DETERMINE EARLY-STAGE VALUATIONS: WINNING THE DEAL

After a VC has decided that they want to invest in your company, the next step is figuring out the valuation they want to offer. There are really only two major considerations – the pre-money valuation and the amount of invested capital, but in order to find the right structure, VC's must balance several additional factors: 1) terms that will win the deal, 2) their target ownership levels and 3) the ownership of other key parties.

Assuming there are structures that are mutually acceptable to both the investor and the entrepreneur, the VC needs to offer both capital levels and a valuation that will get the entrepreneur to accept their offer. In order for an offer to be accepted, it needs to compete with the entrepreneur's other options, including offers from other investors and alternative means of funding the business (e.g., entrepreneur's personal capital, the operation of a cash-generating side businesses, etc).

Selecting a competitive offer requires that a VC understand the market for capital. In other words, they need to have a general understanding of the valuations currently being offered by the other firms at their stage. The valuations offered by competitive firms do fluctuate over time, as a number of exogenous considerations may make investors more or less risk-averse.

Providing the best offer, however, is not the only and often not the most important consideration. VCs need to also ensure that their offer yields appropriate ownership levels for all of the key parties to ensure that their investment is protected.

HOW VCS DETERMINE EARLY STAGE VALUATIONS: TARGET OWNERSHIP

To investors, winning the deal may be less important than protecting their investment. By protecting, I am referring to both the need for incentive alignment in the ownership structure and the VC's need to have an ownership level that provides them with risk-adjusted returns. As a result, VCs are often willing to miss investment opportunities that do not provide them with a sufficient stake in the company.

Professional VCs and angels generally have target ownership levels for their investments. In other words, they have guidelines about the percentage of the company that they expect to own for their invested capital. These ownership levels aren't hard-and-fast numbers, but rather, they are guidelines to help investors avoid drifting too far from their core strategy over time. Generally, these target ranges are simply a reflection of their investment strategy. If you consider the average pre-money valuations at the stage they invest and the size of their typical investment, you can quickly deduce an investor's typical ownership levels.

It is worth noting that since investment strategies do vary by firm, the target ownership levels can differ substantially. Some investors seek to be the sole investor in a company and therefore write a bigger check than investors who prefer to syndicate (share the investment). Those who provide the entire investment often target a greater ownership percentage.

Taking an investment from one firm versus a syndicate does not, however, mean that an entrepreneur will give away more or less of their company – this merely indicates how the new equity is distributed. For example, a single investor could buy 30 percent of the company for $1 million or two investors could each buy 15 percent of the company for $500,000. Either way, 30 percent of the company is sold for $1 million.

While most investors do not have rigid ownership requirements, the designated target ownership levels do serve as an important metric for VCs as they help investors know when to walk away from a deal.

HOW VCS DETERMINE EARLY STAGE VALUATIONS: OWNERSHIP OF KEY PARTIES

I addressed the importance of providing an offer that can win the deal and ensuring that the investor achieves their target ownership levels. The third major consideration that is weighed into the valuation decision is the ownership of key stakeholders.

Investors want managers who are instrumental to the success of the business to have enough equity in the company to ensure incentive alignment. In other words, VCs want to make sure that key managers have enough upside to be motivated to do their best to build the company.

Generally, good investors spend time evaluating investment scenarios to ensure that key managers acquire acceptable ownership levels. By adjusting the pre-money valuation and the amount of capital invested, VCs can adjust the ownership of managers after the investment.

In extreme instances, the company's operators might have far too little equity going into the deal, leaving management with an insignificant ownership percentage after being further diluted by the investment. In these situations, investors may seek to increase the ownership of management in other ways than adjusting the valuation and the amount of invested capital. The most common remedy for this is the issuance of additional options, which are given to key managers. Unfortunately, this approach further dilutes other shareholders (such as angels).

Selecting a venture valuation is a balancing act where a variety of ownership levels need to be balanced. The key to being successful is finding a fair balance that is mutually acceptable, risk adjusted and creates the appropriate incentive alignment.

VCS WANT KEY TEAM MEMBERS TO HAVE A SIGNIFICANT STAKE

When a VC decides to invest, he focuses on structuring both his relationship with the company and the relationship of others within the company in a manner that will increase the odds of success.

To be clear, by success I mean two things:

1. That the VC's position will be protected, and
2. That the company is poised to generate at large exit.

VCs protect their positions through the use of preferred stock structures and other rights. At the end of the day, though, a VC maximizes his chances of top-tier returns not through legal structures but by ensuring that a company's management holds the same goals for the business as a VC.

The basic incentive typically considered during the structuring of the deal is the equity stake of key team members.

At the end of the day, VCs do not run portfolio companies. The best VCs want to make sure that the key members of each management team have a good bit of equity, ensuring that they have significant upside and real incentives to build their company to a scale that generates returns for everyone. It's worth repeating: good VCs want current and future team members to own a significant share of the company.

This premise also holds true when the company is more mature – board members often issue key operators additional options to keep incentives aligned.

This reality doesn't imply that entrepreneurs are sometimes challenged by the ownership requirements of VCs. Entrepreneurs who are less experienced with the venture process may have valuation expectations that are unrealistic given the risk profile and the return requirements of an early stage investment. As a result, VC ownership requirements can surprise newcomers.

However, industry veterans are usually aware of VC ownership requirements, why they exist and the fact that founders can do very well despite not owning the vast majority of a venture-backed company. When a company lives up to its potential, the model typically works – VCs get their returns and entrepreneurs become very wealthy.

In sum, VCs also want entrepreneurs to have a significant stake in the company. However, it's worthwhile to be familiar with the venture capital model, as understanding the typical ownership stakes after a VC investment can ensure that expectations are aligned before term sheets are issued.

The Cap Table

HOW A VC CAN CHANGE THE CAP TABLE

At some point before a VC begins preparing your term sheet, he will ask you to send him a copy of your cap table. There is a right and a wrong way to go about this.

A VC will need your current cap table in order to think through how to structure an investment. Structuring an investment is a balancing act: The VC wants to identify a valuation and investment amount that gives the VC an equity position that meets his investment requirements, but also ensures that the entrepreneur has sufficient incentive to build a big company.

For the most part, cap tables can only be changed by adding new shares – private companies rarely buy back large quantities of stock. Therefore, in order to rebalance the percentage ownership of all stakeholders, VCs propose the creation of new shares which investors purchase. Doing so reduces the percentage of the company that pre-existing shares own, making room for the investor to obtain a share of the company.

However, this reduction doesn't mean that the old shares are worth less. By definition, the new shares are purchased at the share price set in the round; if that price is equal to or higher than the price set in the previous round, the value of the existing shares remains the same or increases with the new price.

In some cases, VCs may want to increase the ownership of key operators as part of the round, providing them with greater incentives. They can do this by issuing new shares, which are granted to operators in the form of options.

In sum, when an investor issues a term sheet it will propose a new cap table that is rebalanced to ensure both that they have a sufficient stake in the company and that incentives are aligned with key managers going forward.

OPTION POOLS

Option pools are common shares that are set aside to compensate and incentivize future employees of the company. The most sophisticated entrepreneurs create option pools before seeking investment from VCs. However whether or not you have created an option pool before seeking investment, the cap table proposed by a VC will include an option pool.

Option pools are created at or before the time of investment for a few reasons:

1. Option pools ensure that the company has sufficient shares to compensate new hires, avoiding any future politicking of stakeholders to protect their investments at the expense of the company's growth.
2. Creating new shares in the future can be costly (legal and accounting fees) and time consuming (as the board is required to meet and approve the creation of new shares).
3. By allocating the option pool up front, it is easier for the VC to evaluate the dilutive effect that these shares might have on stakeholders, enabling VCs to ensure that the cap table is appropriately balanced for the near future.

Depending on how many employees the company needs to hire in the future, their seniority in the company and the value of the company, the size of the option pool may vary. In my experience, however, at the Series A round the option pool is typically sized as 10 to 20 percent of the post-investment cap table.

Options pools are a standard component of the cap table – something that entrepreneurs should be aware of when considering the future structuring of the company.

OPTION POOLS ARE NOT ALWAYS DILUTIVE

One important but often misunderstood characteristic about options is that they do not necessarily dilute shareholders. Options only become shares and dilute existing shareholders if they are exercised. If options are not both allocated and exercised, the shares are never issued and the existing shareholders are not diluted.

This nuance is an important one. Entrepreneurs and investors may disagree about the amount of options required to expand the team and scale the business. You can mitigate the risk of dilution for investors by creating or increasing the option pool prior to investment.

There are a few cases in which options might not be allocated or exercised. If you don't need as much equity to build your team as you planned (and had set aside in the option pool), or if you issue (allocate) options to employees, but they do not exercise the options, you might not allocate all of your options.

Since options that aren't allocated (and aren't exercised) will not dilute other shareholders, if you're negotiating with an investor about the size of an option pool that you believe you'll never use, you might want to pick another battle.

HOW TO CALCULATE SWEAT EQUITY

Many entrepreneurs struggle with determining how much equity to give people who join their team early on. This calculation is often complicated by the fact that many early employees or consultants trade cash compensation for additional equity.

While this calculation is ultimately determined by the negotiation between two parties, I find that a little back-of-the-envelope math can provide some key benchmarks. For companies on path to raise venture capital, the best available starting point for these calculations is the typical equity ownership of employees after a Series A investment. These ownership levels can be adjusted for the likely dilution of a Series A investment to get an estimate of an appropriate equity ownership level for employees engaged before the Series A. Further, since these ownership levels reflect compensation in addition to the cash compensation paid to employees, these benchmarks should probably be adjusted upward to reflect foregone cash.

Companies expecting smaller exit values or differing levels of dilution should adjust the benchmark calculation accordingly.

After you have calculated benchmarks, it's important to sanity check the equity splits to be sure that the cap table is fair to everyone involved.

It is worth noting that the cap table can be changed down the road if the parties on the board or equivalent approve.

MAKE SURE SWEAT EQUITY VESTS

Once you grant equity to an employee, partner or service provider, you can't take it back (without legal action). While you can dilute their ownership by issuing more shares, doing so is difficult and can create a liability for the company.

As a result, it's very important that you make sure to vest every equity grant that you make – giving the recipient rights to more equity as they achieve milestones. Doing so enables you to pull the plug on the relationship at any point down the road to prevent the recipient from receiving more equity.

While equity can vest based upon milestones, such as the acquisition of a key partner, meeting sales targets or the development of a product, time is the most commonly used determinant of vesting. Employees and founders vest their equity over a pre-defined period of time. Most often this is a three- to six- year period, whereby vesting occurs on a monthly basis.

Some structures will include a "vesting cliff." Before the cliff, no equity vests. At the time of the cliff, the recipient catches up on his vesting so that it is as though there was no cliff. For example if an employee is set to vest on an equal monthly basis over four years but has a one-year cliff, he would receive no equity until the end of 12 months at which time he would receive 12 months worth of vesting – in this case 25 percent of the total grant. Cliffs are very useful tools for founders as they provide a trial period. If an employee or partner doesn't work out before the end of the cliff, the company can part ways with the recipient of the grant without giving him any equity.

Many first-time entrepreneurs give away equity to people who don't do much to earn it. A vesting schedule with a cliff can help prevent this.

WHY EMPLOYEES RECEIVE COMMON STOCK

When employees are granted stock, or more often stock options, they are entitled to shares of common stock. Common stock offers employees access to the economic benefits of ownership, aligning incentives to focus on increasing the value of the company.

It's worth noting that these option plans do not provide employees with preferred stock for several key reasons.

First, preferred stock is designed to offer its holders unique control over specific aspects of corporate decisions (e.g., sale of the company, compensation of senior executives, etc.). These aren't decisions that employees are in a position to make, as they aren't always privy to all of the information required to make these decisions.

Second, investors seek preferred stock because it enables them to make the aforementioned decisions. When those decisions need to be made, a vote is taken amongst the holders of preferred stock. By giving employees preferred stock, investors would own a smaller percentage of the total pool of preferred stock, reducing their ability to control these votes. As a result, the distribution of preferred stock would prevent investors from providing the company with capital.

In sum, employees are granted common stock because it is designed to offer them the incentive to exclusively focus on expanding the value of the company.

Preferred Stock

PREFERRED STOCK

When venture investors make an investment, they buy a new class of shares that are created by the company. These shares are designed to have different rights than common shares (the shares that are initially created by the company).

These rights are created to protect the investment for the investor, which usually involves obtaining control over decisions in relatively extreme situations and structuring aspects of the company's finances to ensure that management and the investors have aligned incentives.

While some investors like to create special rights, by and large these structures are relatively boilerplate. At their core, many investors offer essentially the same terms and have been doing so for several decades.

PREFERRED STOCK: PARTICIPATION

The breed of preferred stock most often used by VCs is called participating preferred. The word participating refers to a specific feature of the stock: its ability to convert to common during attractive exit events.

This is an important aspect as it ensures that the owners of the stock are able to get a cut of exit proceeds allocated to the equity pool in proportion to their ownership levels. In plain English, this means that if the participating preferred holders have 25 percent of the shares in the company they will typically get 25 percent of the proceeds made available to the common stock pool.

It's worth noting that the portion that is available to the common stock holders is not the total exit value of the company as other stakeholders, such as lenders, typically get paid before the common equity holders.

PREFERRED STOCK: LIQUIDITY PREFERENCE

I mentioned that there is a hierarchy that determines the order in which parties get paid when a company is sold. The first group to get paid is the lenders, often followed by equity holders. Within the equity holders there can also be a hierarchy; determining which types of equity holders get paid first. Preferred stock typically includes a liquidity preference that is paid before common stock.

In most scenarios, the liquidity preference gives preferred stock holders the right to get paid out a fixed amount – usually a multiple of their total dollars invested – before common stock is paid. For example, if an investor has a one-times liquidity preference, they will get that money back before capital is allocated to the common pool.

It is important to note that liquidity preference is in addition to participation. As a result, investors get a multiple of their money back and then have rights to their percentage of the payout to common stockholders.

HOW LIQUIDITY PREFERENCE IMPACTS INVESTOR RETURNS

It's important to think about how the payout structure impacts returns for an investor. Since its impact on returns varies with the exit value, the best way to demonstrate this is through a few scenarios.

To isolate the impact of the liquidity preference we're going to assume two things:

1. That this company only takes in one round of investment, and
2. The capital structure is very simple – the company only has preferred stock and common stock.

Let's assume that the pre-money valuation for this investment was $5 million and the new equity was $2.5 million, yielding a post-money value of $7.5 million. In this scenario, let's assume that the liquidity preference is one times new equity.

This scenario results in the common (e.g., founders, angels, etc.) owning 66 percent ($5 million / $7.5 million) of the company and the investors owning 33 percent ($2.5 million / $7.5 million).

Exit Scenario 1: Downside Case

Here's what happens if the company sells for $10 million.

The investors would take their liquidity preference of $2.5 million (their initial investment) off of the top, leaving $7.5 million to the common pool. The preferred stockholders (the investors) and the common stockholders (founders, angels, etc.) would then divvy up the remaining capital according to their ownership percentage. The investors would get 33 percent of $7.5 million or $2.5 million and the common stockholders would get 66 percent of the $7.5 million or $5 million.

Bottom line: The investors would receive $2.5 million from their liquidity preference and $2.5 million from their participation. This is a $5 million payout, which doubles their initial investment. Note that the liquidity preference represented 50 percent of returned capital.

Exit Scenario 2: Upside Case

Now let's assume that the company exits for $100 million.

The investors would take their liquidity preference of $2.5 million (their initial investment) off of the top, leaving $97.5 million to the common pool. The preferred stockholders (the investors) and the common stockholders (founders, angels, etc.) would then divvy up the remaining capital according to their ownership percentage. The investors would get 33 percent of $97.5 million or $32.5 million and the common stockholders would get 66 percent of the $97.5 million or $65 million.

In sum, the investors would receive $2.5 million from their liquidity preference and $32.5 million from their participation. This is a $35 million payout, which gives them a 14-times return on their initial investment. Note that the liquidity preference represented 7 percent of returned capital.

The scenarios above highlight the impact of the liquidity preference on investor returns. Simply put, it has less of an impact as the exit value of the company increases. The real returns in a venture portfolio are generated through the participation in the common stock pool.

WHY LIQUIDITY PREFERENCE EXISTS

It's common to hear participating preferred stock (which has a liquidity preference and participation rights) referred to as a sneaky way to increase returns. However, liquidity preference has a smaller impact on returns as exit values increase. While the liquidity preference does increase returns for investors, if that were the only objective, there are better ways to achieve it. Most obviously, returns on any given investment could be more effectively increased by negotiating lower pre-money valuations, enabling investors to have a greater participation in the upside when big exits happen. The potential additional payout from having more upside would very likely outweigh the downside protection that the liquidity preference provides.

This begs the question, how much downside protection does the liquidity preference provide investors? In the downside scenario I mention previously, the liquidity preference plays a key role, accounting for 50 percent of the returned capital. However, not all companies have a $10 million exit – many go to zero. Without an exit event, liquidity preference doesn't do much.

This leaves us asking ourselves, if liquidity preference has a relatively small impact on the upside and is not frequently leveraged on the downside, why is it used?

The main reason is incentive alignment. Liquidity preference ensures that the entrepreneurs are focused on realizing a big exit. Early stage VCs invest in companies because they believe they can exit for several hundred million dollars or more. Without the liquidity preference, entrepreneurs may be tempted to pursue $10 million exits – seeking a $5 million personal payout before they realize the full potential of the company. Liquidity preference enables investors to get their money back first in those situations, reducing the payout to the entrepreneurs and keeping them enticed to seek the $100 million exit. Through liquidity preference the incentives are aligned; no one does well when the exits are small and everyone makes a lot of money when the exits are big.

This isn't to say that the impact of liquidity preference on returns in small exits isn't important – it can be for an individual investment. However, the impact of liquidity preference on a VC's overall fund return probably isn't extremely significant. In contrast, making sure that entrepreneurs are focused on making big companies always matters. My point here is that the main purpose of this structure is to align the incentives between investors and entrepreneurs, keeping everyone focused on making something really big.

LIQUIDITY PREFERENCE IS ACCRETIVE

Investors in each round of funding are likely to require a liquidity preference, meaning that Series A, Series B and Series C investors may each have their own liquidity preferences that need to be paid out before common. As a result, when another round of investment is made, the total liquidity preference typically increases.

While this might seem daunting to entrepreneurs at first read, it is usually palatable. The company is typically closer to realizing a high exit valuation (which more than covers that liquidity preference) with each subsequent round of investment.

WHY LIQUIDITY PREFERENCE MAY VARY

VCs and most other investors usually reserve the right to get their invested capital paid back through the proceeds of an exit before common shareholders divvy up any remaining payout. What I didn't mention earlier is that the amount that a VC has a right to be paid back may vary.

The value of a VC's liquidity preference is typically measured as a multiple of the capital invested. A 1x liquidity preference entitles the VC to get paid one dollar before common for every dollar that the VC invests. At a 2x, for every dollar of invested capital the VC has the right to get paid two dollars back before the remaining payout is divided amongst common.

In a healthy market, an average risk investment will be offered a 1x liquidity preference. However, several factors may drive up liquidity preference.

Downside Protection

While liquidity preference is most effective for aligning incentives, it can also be used to increase downside protection. While no one gets paid if no exit takes place, an increased liquidity preference can increase the payout for an investor in a small exit scenario. As a result, when there is a lot of systematic (market) risk affecting startups or a particular startup is a uniquely risky venture (idiosyncratic risk) a VC may hedge the bet a little bit by requiring a higher liquidity preference multiple.

This was a common technique used during the recession following the bust of the Internet bubble. Startups were less likely to reach their potential due to several market risks: limited available capital for high tech companies and recessionary customer spending habits. Therefore, VCs increased their required liquidity preferences in order to mitigate some of the downside associated with smaller exits.

MARKET DYNAMICS KEEP LIQUIDITY PREFERENCE IN CHECK

It's worth noting that VCs do not operate in a vacuum – if other investors are willing to offer lower liquidity preference multiples, then the higher multiples won't make it to the market. As a result, multiples are likely only to vary (with any frequency) when there is a market-wide shift in investor expectations.

But, some VCs will require a higher liquidity preference for a specific deal – they simply may not want to do the deal without the higher preference. However, if other VCs are interested, the entrepreneur may be able to work with investors who do not have the same liquidity preference requirements.

Other Terms

VCS GENERALLY RETAIN PRO-RATA RIGHTS (RIGHT OF FIRST REFUSAL)

Most VC term sheets give them pro-rata investment rights, not the right to purchase all of the issued shares.

In many cases VCs seek outside (new) investors to lead subsequent rounds of financing of a company. While the economic incentives for having an outsider lead the round vary by fund size, outsiders are often sought to lead new financing rounds because they can provide additional contacts for management and external validation of the company's valuation.

The valuation provided by an inside (existing) investor is not considered to be as solid of a market number as insiders have an incentive to both minimize and maximize the price of the round, creating a dynamic that leads to less reliable market valuations. At a higher valuation, the insider protects their existing investment from dilution and at a lower valuation they are able to buy shares at a lower price. They have conflicting incentives.

The external valuation is important for investor bookkeeping, setting prices for options and warrants, and negotiating exit valuations.

As a result, most VC term sheets give them only the right to make their pro-rata investment, not the right to lead subsequent rounds. This right is referred to as the right of first refusal.

So, what is pro-rata? It's best to explain with an example.

If the company wants to raise an additional $10 million of capital, they may find a lead investor who is only willing to provide $5 million of the round. The remaining $5 million dollars may be made available to the insiders (existing investors). The $10 million would be split 50/50 – $5 million from the outsider (new) investor and $5 million from the insider (existing) investors.

Each of the existing insiders would have the option to invest up to their pro-rata percentage of the inside portion. The pro-rata percentage is defined as the percentage of the total capital already invested in the company that they provided. Let's assume a VC had invested 20 percent of the total capital taken in by the company prior to this new round. This VC would then have the option to invest up to 20 percent of the $5 million inside round – or $1 million.

There are some nuances to this. Not all investors are granted pro-rata rights and investors usually have the option to invest more if other insiders elect not to make their pro-rata investment.

In sum, VCs don't usually have a call option on the next round in a typical venture round (Series A, Series B or beyond).

PRO-RATA STILL DILUTES VCS

One implication of the fact that insider investors generally do not provide all of the invested capital in future rounds is that insiders can be diluted; inside investors own a smaller percentage of the company after subsequent investments. While the value of their ownership should (in theory) be worth more as more capital is invested, VCs generally see their ownership stake decline over the life of the company.

What determines whether or not the insiders are diluted is the relationship between the percentage of the company owned by insiders before the round relative to the percentage of the newly issued shares that they acquire in the round. Simply put, existing investors need to acquire a percentage of newly issued shares equal to their pre-existing ownership percentage to maintain their ownership level in the company. If they acquire a greater percentage of new shares, their ownership will increase. If they acquire a smaller percentage of new shares, their ownership will decrease.

Here are a few examples of the math in action.

No Dilution

Note that two light green cells in the model are the same. Venture Co. is receiving a percentage of the round equal to their pre-existing ownership percentage – therefore there is no dilution.

Dilutive

In the example below, the outsider provides a larger percentage of the invested capital in the new round, resulting in dilution for the existing investors. Note that this is the common scenario in the development of a healthy company (when the existing investors intend to provide a minority of the portfolio company's invested capital). Venture Co.'s ownership percentage declines from 25 percent to 21 percent.

Anti-Dilutive

In this scenario the inside investors provide the majority of the invested capital. This scenario is most likely to take place when there is an existing investor who seeks to provide the majority of the company's invested capital, when the existing investors believe that the market is undervaluing the company or when there is not an interested outside investor. Note that Venture Co. increases its ownership through this investment.

NO ONE LIKES TO BE LEFT OUT: CO-SALE RIGHTS

VCs generally require co-sale rights when they make an investment. This right enables them to participate in any sale or transfer of stock to a third party.

This term enables investors to avoid missing out on opportunities to liquidate their shares. The founders or a sub-set of the company's shareholders can't secretly find buyers willing to pay a high price for their shares and engage in the transaction without giving their VCs the right to participate.

DIVIDENDS: COMMON STRUCTURES

Term sheets may include some provision for dividends to be paid to the investor. These dividends are commonly structured in one of three ways: when declared, cumulative and compound.

When Declared

In this structure, investors only get dividends when the board declares a dividend for the firm. The legal language will often ensure that a dividend cannot be paid to another share class without also paying the same dividend to the preferred shareholders (investors). To be clear, if the board doesn't declare a dividend, then one isn't paid. If the board does declare a dividend, the investors get to participate.

Cumulative

Another common structure is for the investor to require that an annual dividend be paid to them. Usually the dividend amount is a percentage of their initial investment.

Most early-stage companies do not have excess cash to pay dividends, however. If they do generate excess cash, they typically re-invest it into the company. As a result, investors accumulate their dividends as liquidity preference, to be paid before common shareholders get to participate.

Compounding

Compounding dividends are structured much like cumulative dividends. They are paid based on a predetermined percentage and accumulate as liquidity preference. Compounding dividends differ in that the annual dividend amount is not determined as a percentage of initial investment, it is determined as a percentage of the initial investment plus the total accrued dividends. Investors are paid dividends on dividends.

WHY VCS TAKE DIVIDENDS

As aforementioned, there are three commonly used structures by which VCs accrue dividends. The motivation to use each of these dividend structures varies.

When Declared

The when declared structure is designed to ensure that the VCs aren't excluded from dividend payments. This prevents the board from declaring dividends that only pay other share classes and leave the VCs out.

Cumulative

Cumulative dividends enable VCs to be compensated for investments that take longer to liquidate. From an investor perspective, this makes sense as the longer it takes to realize an investment (have the company exit) the worse their returns looks to the investors in the venture capital fund. As a result, by accruing dividends a VC's return can be enhanced, partially offsetting the effect of having a longer duration to liquidation.

Compounding

Compounding dividends can substantially increase investor returns over time. While some VCs will use this structure simply to enhance returns, this approach may also be used to create incentive alignment. In unique situations where there is either 1) additional risk to holding onto an investment for an extended period (e.g., a patent expiring) or 2) where there is concern that the entrepreneur will not be seeking an appropriately timed exit.

In the situation of the patent expiration, the value of the exit may decline over time. Having compounding dividends enables an investor to increase their liquidity preference, thereby increasing the percentage of the exit value that they will have rights to as the company's value declines. This may have the effect of stabilizing a return. Conversely, in this scenario the operators will receive a smaller percentage of the payout as time passes, creating an incentive from them to sell the company early.

In the second situation, where the investors are concerned about the entrepreneur's intent to pursue an exit, the compounding dividends does create an incentive for the entrepreneur to consider the timing of the sale (in addition to the size of the exit).

It's worth noting that it's most common to see the when declared or cumulative dividend structures in term sheets.

ANTI-DILUTION: TAKING COVER

When everything goes to plan, the value of your company will increase in each subsequent round of investment. If your company was valued at $10 million (including the invested capital) after the last round, you might hope that the company is valued at $20 million by the next round. In theory, this is the natural order of the venture world. Entrepreneurs take capital and create value, making the company worth more than it was before.

Unfortunately, we live in a messy world where reality and theory diverge. In some instances a company will be worth less at the time it is seeking its next round of capital. The company that was once worth $10 million may now only be worth $5 million.

This change in value can occur for any number of reasons. The company's revenue model may not have panned out as planned, a key customer defected or a critical partnership may have fallen apart, leaving the intrinsic value of the company to be worth less than it was before. Alternatively, the market for venture capital tends to ebb and flow. When capital is in short supply the valuations of company's may decline if the company was overvalued.

Whatever the cause, down-rounds (rounds in which the company is devalued relative to a prior round) do happen and investors know this. When down-rounds take place, the existing shareholders of the company before the investment (founders, staff and investors) often experience a significant decline in the percentage of the company that they own. As a result, VCs often require that companies accept anti-dilution provisions that protect their ownership stake when the company is devalued. When a down-round takes place, these terms effectively decrease the ownership percentage of the founders and the staff more significantly than the ownership percentage of the investors.

This protects VCs and their investors from crisis scenarios where assumptions made by management prove to be inaccurate or when the company's proved to be unsustainable as the capital market fluctuates.

COMMON ANTI-DILUTION STRUCTURES

Anti-dilution terms protect an investor's ownership percentage if the value of its shares declines in a financing round relative to a previous round. These terms provide formulas for calculating an investor's ownership if the company raises additional capital at a lower valuation.

There are two commonly used anti-dilution structures: broad-based weighted average and full-ratchet. The math associated with each of these scenarios is somewhat complicated; your lawyer should be able to ensure that the methodology proposed is industry standard. What you need to understand is the conceptual impact of the terms on the other shareholders in these situations.

Broad-Based Weighted Average

While broad-based weighted average anti-dilution (also referred to as weighted average anti-dilution) effectively reduces the percentage ownership of an investor, the investor's ownership percentage declines by less than the percentage by which the value of the
company declined.

This has an important implication for you as the entrepreneur. First, you should understand that the presence of anti-dilution provisions will result in your ownership being disproportionately diluted in down rounds. If you are key to the company's operation, subsequent to a highly dilutive financing, the board may elect to issue you additional options to keep you motivated. You should be careful about raising capital at a valuation that is not sustainable in more typical fundraising environments if you expect to need additional capital in the future and are raising money in a boom period in the venture market.

Broad-based weighted average dilution is a commonplace term used in the industry by sophisticated investors.

Full-Ratchet

The full-ratchet anti-dilution term maintains the value of the investor's investment in the event of a down-round. Simply put, if the VC invested $1 million at $1 per share (giving them an ownership of 1 million shares) and the company's value is cut in half, the VC would then own 2 million shares that are valued at $0.50 a share. The value of their ownership remains consistent.

The impact of this provision on other shareholders is severe in highly dilutive situations, substantially increasing the effective dilution of down rounds on other shareholders.

This term is less commonly seen in deal documents than weighted average anti-dilution. It does, however, have a role in the investor ecosystem. In situations where entrepreneurs have sought very aggressive valuations, investors may require the right of full-ratchet anti-dilution protection to ensure that their investment is protected if the company's valuation proves unsustainable.

REDEMPTION RIGHTS: RECOVERING INVESTMENT

Venture capitalists invest in startup companies with the expectation of realizing an exit in order to pay back their limited partners. In some situations, however, management may not be as focused on realizing an exit as there may be incentive misalignment when it comes to liquidating the company. This is most likely to happen in situations where 1) the company is generating enough cash to make the founders wealthy from dividend payments or 2) the management team does not have the right mix of options in their compensating plan, leaving either party with less incentive to aggressively pursue an exit.

Therefore, VCs often require that they receive redemption rights when they invest. These rights enable the investors to force the company to buy the investor's shares back from them after a specified period of time for a specified value. The specified period of time is often a period that is sufficient for the company to pursue an exit if the company performs (often five years or more). This is an important point, as this term is not designed in spirit to provide VCs with early liquidity, but rather to give the VCs a means of realizing liquidity if an exit has not been pursued. The value of the equity is often the fair market value at the time that the redemption is enacted.

These rights are commonplace and shouldn't be cause for concern for entrepreneurs who intend to exit their company. If it is your intention to maintain an independent, private entity in perpetuity, never giving your investors a liquidity event, however, you should communicate that to your investors before taking their money and you should not seek traditional venture capital.

WILL VCS REIMBURSE YOUR STARTUP EXPENSES?

When you raise money from VCs, you're taking in capital to support the operations of the company. Some entrepreneurs may wonder, however, if expenses incurred before the funding are also covered by the capital. Can VC money be used to reimburse founders or prior investors for their expenses?

The answer to this is generally no. VCs are investing in the company to drive it forward and they're pretty keen on their investment being used only for future expenses. There's good reason for this. First, VCs want to ensure that more money stays in the company to extend the runway and increase the probability of the company succeeding. Second, investors usually like to see founders keep some skin in the game. Prior investments of time and capital further align a founder's incentives with that of the investors.

So, how is someone compensated for money they put into the company before raising VC? Through equity. The valuation at which the VCs invest reflects the total value of the company inclusive of the value of the idea, the commitment of the team and prior capital investments. Money invested in the company should increase the company's valuation, leaving the founders with more ownership in the company. So, like VCs, founders receive equity for their capital.

In general, when you invest money in your startup, assume that you are doing so to increase its value, not to get paid back.

DEAL TERMS: CONTROL

Governance

HOW COMPANIES ARE GOVERNED

In order to understand how much control a VC will have over your company once you've accepted an investment, you will first need to understand how companies are controlled.

There are as many ways to control a company as there are to skin a cat. Control mechanisms can be segmented into two approaches: formal corporate governance and non-traditional tactics. Broadly speaking, non-traditional tactics include everything not baked into the governing documents of the corporation. These tactics might range from leveraging contracts, holding code hostage and taking legal action to illicit activity.

While venture investors are keenly aware of non-traditional tactics (since they will see to ensure that none are being used), they will assert their control through formal corporate governance.

According to dictionary.com, corporate governance is "the relationship between all the stakeholders in a company. This includes the shareholders, directors, and management of a company, as defined by the corporate charter, bylaws, formal policy, and rule of law". In practical terms, corporate governance generally refers to the rules created to determine how decisions are made in a company.

At a high level, after a VC invests in your company, big-picture decisions are made in one of three ways:

1. **Common Shareholders:** All of the shareholders vote (usually preferred shareholders participate in an as-if-converted-to-common basis) and if a proposal receives a vote exceeding the minimum pre-defined threshold for approval (e.g., majority or two-thirds), then it is approved. This approach is the most commonly understood by people in business.

2. **Board:** Other decisions are made by the board of directors. In this method, if the required percentage of the board votes in favor of a proposal it is approved.

3. **Preferred Shareholders:** Some decisions are made solely based upon a vote by a specified class of shares. In these situations, if at least the minimum required percentage of shares in the specified share class vote in favor of the proposal, it is passed.

At a high level, these three mechanisms drive most of the key decisions in a venture-backed startup. With this understanding of control mechanisms, we can dive more deeply into how VCs control startups in the ensuing segments.

WHY IS GOVERNANCE IMPORTANT?

When companies take their first institutional investment, they usually have little in the way of corporate governance. For many companies, at the early stage decisions are simply made by the founder(s) with no formal vote at all. While these companies might have a board of advisers, their board is generally there merely to advise, not direct.

All of this changes when a startup takes an investment from a VC. Good VCs require their portfolio companies to put in place robust corporate governance structures, decision making procedures, disaggregated control (e.g., a board of directors), etc.

For some this may beg the question, "Why does governance matter?"

Ultimately, governance enables a corporation to improve its ability to make decisions that maximize overall shareholder value. In practice, this means enabling the company to work through stalemates and protect minority investors when incentives are not aligned. In other words, governance stabilizes a company, enabling it to better weather complicated decisions. For VCs, governance protects their investments by reducing the odds that challenging decisions will destroy the company.

Governance is not only important for internal decision-making, it is also important for shaping external perceptions. Partners and customers want to work with companies that are positioned to continue to provide services for the duration of their relationship. While early-stage companies do face a litany of risks, having proper governance in place can mitigate the risk that internal conflicts will implode the company. A VC investment is often seen as a "good housekeeping seal of approval."

As a result, the governance that VCs bring to startups increases the odds that a startup can both survive difficult decisions and more easily engage in contracts with customers and partners.

DAY-TO-DAY DECISIONS ARE MADE BY MANAGEMENT

To clarify, not all corporate decisions are made by one of the three decision-making mechanisms: a vote of the preferred shareholders, common shareholders or the board. This would make for a pretty slow decision making process, hampering the development of the company. The day-to-day decisions are made by the management team.

I use the word "key" to describe decisions that are not solely made by management. So what makes something a key decision? Ultimately, key – an intentionally vague word – is used to imply that the decision is viewed as important to the investor.

Important decisions include (but are not limited to) decisions about the company's financing (raising new capital, taking on debt, etc.), capital structure (issuing new shares, etc.) and strategic plans (e.g., joint ventures, significant capital expenditures, exits, etc.).

In practice, the investors, management, and their lawyers identify which decisions will be made by management and which will be made by one of the other three decision mechanisms. While numerous types of decisions need to be categorized, the process isn't as tedious as it might sound. Professional investors and experienced lawyers have created enough governance structures over the past decades to build a robust knowledge base and a relatively standardized set of rules for corporate decision making. As a result, while there is some variance by law firm and investors, the process of finalizing the governance structure is usually limited to a process of tweaking and refining the rules, rather than creating them anew.

Many of these decision-making structures are proposed in an investor term sheet and made official through a shareholders agreement.

INVESTORS TYPICALLY PARTICIPATE IN ALL THREE DECISION MECHANISMS

An important point to clarify is that early-stage investors typically participate in all three corporate control mechanisms: a vote of the common, of the board or of the preferred shareholders.

If they have preferred shares, which most VCs do, they will have the ability to participate in a vote of the preferred. VCs also often have a board seat in the company (at least until subsequent financing events) enabling them to participate in board votes. Additionally, the votes of the common include preferred shareholders on an as-if-converted basis, meaning that preferred shareholders are entitled to vote for each common share that they would have if they converted at the time of the vote.

HOW VCS CONTROL COMPANIES

VCs generally take minority stakes in the companies in which they invest, so they don't usually have the infamous majority vote.

So how do they maintain enough control to protect their investment? Here's the trick.

I describe earlier the three mechanisms by which major corporate decisions are made: vote of common shareholders, vote of the board members and vote of the preferred shareholders.

By and large, these are sorted by the degree of control that each mechanism gives the VC. VCs have the least control when a vote goes to all of the common shareholders and the most when only the preferred shareholders get to vote. This is simply because VCs inevitably own a larger percentage of the preferred shares than they do the total shares in the company.

As a result, VCs seek to have the most important decisions determined by a vote of the preferred. When I say the most important decisions, I am largely referring to decisions that impact the return on a VC's investment, such as issuing new shares and selling the company. This decision-making structure gives VCs the sway they need to protect their investment while only owning a minority stake in the company.

THE MARKET FOR CONTROL

VCs have more control over decisions when they are put to a vote of the preferred shareholders. One might wonder, "Do VCs require that all decisions are put to a vote of preferred shareholders?" While every VC likely offers slightly different terms, the answer to this is generally no.

The past decades of negotiations between entrepreneurs and VCs have yielded some market norms about how companies are controlled. To a degree, key decisions are generally made in the same way across companies.

The norms that have developed tend to reserve decisions deemed most sensitive to investors for a vote by the preferred shareholders, leaving the majority of key decisions to a vote of the board.

The market for control has matured, significantly reducing the amount of arm wrestling left to do when you take VC money.

VCS MAINTAIN A VOICE BY SETTING THRESHOLDS

Each mechanism of corporate control, whether it be a vote of the common, the board or the preferred shareholders, requires that a certain percentage of the voting population vote in favor of a proposal in order for it to be passed. In a vote of the common and preferred shareholders, each share gets a vote; in a vote of the board, each board seat gets a vote.

Proposals are passed when a pre-specified percentage of votes is obtained. In some instances this means a majority vote, in others it could be a seemingly arbitrary number such as 65 percent. While to some this threshold for approval might appear to be a secondary consideration, it is an important number as it determines which parties are required to vote in favor of a proposal for it to be approved.

In most cases, early-stage investors are not poised to pass a proposal in a vote of the common or the board without the vote of another party, such as the CEO or the largest shareholder. These thresholds, however, can ensure that the vote of the VCs is required to approve decisions in these situations. While they won't be able to approve proposals unilaterally, they may be able to stop others from doing so.

Just as the mechanism for decision-making can vary by type of decision, so can thresholds. These thresholds are typically proposed in the term sheet and made official in the shareholder's agreement.

While VCs can't predict what types of decisions will need to be made in the future and how the various constituencies will support or oppose them, these thresholds can enable VCs to remain relevant in the decision-making process.

WHO CARES ABOUT MAJORITY OWNERSHIP, ANYWAY?

I often hear entrepreneurs express concern about not owning a majority of the stock in their company. Typically they're worried about losing control as they give away equity to expand their team, secure partnerships and raise capital. Crossing the halfway point in the company seems to be a scary milestone for some founders.

In practice, however, there may not be a whole lot of difference for an entrepreneur between owning 51 percent and 49 percent (or less) of their company. Moreover, many founders give away meaningful control long before they stop holding their majority stake or maintain meaningful control long after.

The three ways in which key decisions are made within a corporation are by a vote of the preferred shareholders, board of directors and the common shareholders. The remainder of the day-to-day decisions are made by the management team which may or may not include the founder.

Owning a majority stake in the company (which means owning a majority of the common shares) really only gives the entrepreneur veto power over decisions put to a vote of the common. This likely represents not only a small percentage of the company's decisions, but also a minor share of the decisions that the entrepreneur cares about, such as exit plans and setting the company's overall strategy.

As a result, I generally find the fear of losing a majority stake to be more emotional than practical – having a majority share of common often does not give the entrepreneur meaningful control of the company.

HOW TO STAY IN CONTROL OF YOUR COMPANY

Having majority ownership of a company's common stock typically doesn't necessitate having control over the company's key decisions. Since a vote of the common shareholders is just one of the three mechanisms by which key decisions are made in corporations, a majority owner of common could lose control through the other two voting mechanisms. To be clear, a shareholder can lose control of a corporation despite having a majority of the company's common stock or, conversely, stay in control of the company with only a minority stake. It all boils down to positioning across the three decision-making mechanisms.

This begs the question, "How can you maintain influence in key decisions made through all three mechanisms?"

There is no easy answer to this, as your ability to maintain influence is often a function of the negotiating leverage you have with potential partners (investors, employees or others). Obviously, the less you need what your partner is offering (e.g., capital, expertise, etc.) and the more they want to be a part of your venture, the more likely you are to be able to obtain terms that leave you with control of your company. In this extreme case you could give yourself special shares with more common votes than those allocated to your partner, disband the board of directors and eliminate a vote of the preferred shareholders. In practice, however, few negotiations can be characterized by an extremely asymmetric balance of power, leaving both parties to compromise. As a result, shareholders are often left to seek control of companies within the typical control structures.

This means seeking the best possible position in each of the three control structures. There are, however, some tactics that entrepreneurs can employ to improve their influence in each control structure.

Vote of the Common

In theory, founders maximize their positioning in the vote of the common by ensuring that they can influence the greatest percentage of the common votes as possible. In practice, this means selling the least amount of equity possible. Often this can mean acquiring as few resources as possible (capital and talent) as late as possible in the life of the company – when the company's value has appreciated.

It is important for founders to remember that they may be able to influence more shares that they own directly. The votes of allies can provide founders with more leverage, often giving them the boost they need to win a contested decision.

Vote of the Board of Directors

Similarly, founders often seek to influence board decisions through allies. By filling board seats with "yes-men" or people with aligned incentives or similar ideology, founders can acquire the votes that they need to influence the direction of the company.

Vote of the Preferred Shareholders

Lastly, founders can seek to increase their role in a vote of the preferred shareholders by co-investing in the company to obtain preferred voting rights. Additionally, entrepreneurs can mitigate the power of the preferred shareholders by negotiating for key decisions to be made by other mechanisms than a vote of the preferred shareholders. Simply put, by having more decisions made by mechanisms where they have influence, founders can exert more control.

It is important to note that sophisticated investors are aware of these tactics and will see them coming.

Seeking a fair deal with regard to both the economics and control of the company is important and worthwhile. If you have reasonable expectations and are working with a good partner, however, these conversations shouldn't be too painful as many of the terms and structures offered in these deals are increasingly boilerplate. In other words, the ending control structure of the company isn't something that is likely to vary too greatly from deal to deal.

BOARD STRUCTURE: SEEKING BALANCE

The composition of the board can greatly impact the level of control of a given party. For example, if it takes a majority of the board's vote to make decisions, if a single party were to control a majority of the seats they would be able to unilaterally make decisions.

As you can see, identifying an appropriate board structure is very important for ensuring that decisions made at the board level are done so with the intention of maximizing shareholder value, not serving the interest of a single party (whether that's a particular investor, executive or founder). Investors, entrepreneurs and employees are all in a venture together and decisions need to be made that attempt to maximize value for all of these parties.

Generally, this is achieved through the creation of a balanced board. A balanced board is a structure that is theoretically designed to prevent either the founders/management or the investors from having a controlling position on the board. This means giving investors and management an equal share of seats on the board. If the investors have two seats then the management might also have two.

At the highest level, the concept of a balanced board is designed to distribute power equally across the interests of the company's key constituencies.

INDEPENDENT DIRECTOR: THE TIE BREAKER

When complicated situations arise, board members may have divergent incentives and perspectives. For example, the board members representing management may want to accept an offer to invest in the company while the investor board members may not. These situations will inevitably develop over time – every board is bound vote on contentious issues. While you can't avoid these topics, you can structure your board to ensure that complicated decisions do not paralyze your company.

Ultimately, the worst scenario for a board is often a stalemate where the board is evenly split on a decision. It's important that your board can make difficult decisions, enabling the company to continue to grow and evolve. The tactic for avoiding this problem is simply to create a board with an odd number of directors. A board of three, five, seven or nine directors virtually ensures that decisions will be made and stalemates avoided.

But how does a board maintain balance between investors and management with an odd number of seats? The odd man out should be an independent.

An independent director, also known as an outside director, is an individual with sufficient understanding of the business so as to help make competent decisions and provides the deciding vote in situations where the management and investor directors are split on an issue. This individual is supposed to be the unbiased voice.

The independent director can be more than the tie-breaking vote, however. Independent directors can be industry experts who provide nuanced insight and a deep Rolodex to the company.

When you are negotiating your term sheet, make sure you structure the board to include the tie-breaking vote.

SECURING AN INDEPENDENT: IDENTIFY CANDIDATES

It can sometimes be more challenging than expected to secure an independent board member. There are two steps involved – identifying interested candidates and then approving them. It's important to think about these two steps when you are navigating the fundraising process.

Identifying independent board members is sometimes easy and sometimes not. Independent directors are motivated to join the boards of startups for a variety of reasons. Often they simply want to stay in the game (if they have retired) or they simply want to further their credentials and credibility in a specific industry. The more the prospective board members are focused on the latter (building their domain expertise and credibility), the more they're going to need to believe in the prospects of the company. The younger your company, the more vision the prospective board member will need to have in order to get excited enough to join the venture.

A good management team pursuing a great idea that is backed by credible investors generally should appeal to potential independents. Despite that, there are times when startups with the right profile have a difficult time identifying interested independents. Often this happens when the company is still very early in its development and has yet to demonstrate traction or when there are few people with the required expertise to join the board, reducing the odds of finding a match.

As a result, it is worthwhile to think about potential independent board members early on in the fundraising process. Having some ideas about who might join the board helps take another small bit of friction out of building the company, making it slightly easier for investors to get comfortable.

PENALTIES FOR NOT SELECTING AN INDEPENDENT

While identifying prospective independent board members will help make VCs more comfortable investing in your startup, they may still be concerned about getting an independent approved.

Selecting independent board members is often done by a process of mutual approval, whereby both the directors representing the management team and the investors must submit approval. This selection process is designed in spirit to ensure that the independent director does not favor one side or the other (they should remain independent of the influences of either party). Nobody wants the other side to have a ringer.

Since independents must receive mutual approval be to be accepted, VCs are sometimes concerned that the management representation on the board will choose to block all of the proposed independents leaving the company with an even number of directors and no mechanisms for breaking ties in the future. While this doesn't happen if all parties are acting in good faith, being a good partner is not always a high priority for individuals.

VCs may therefore seek to insert penalties in the term sheet that incentivize the management side of the board to select an independent director. These terms might include something as aggressive as the VCs taking control of the independent's board seat after a designated period of time and lasting until an independent is selected.

In sum, it's important to VCs that your company selects independent board members. Typically this comes about through a good faith effort by all of the parties. VCs who have had problems securing an independent director in the past may look for mechanisms to ensure that the management team actively works to find and approve this person.

DON'T LET YOUR BOARD GET TOO CROWDED

At first glance, it may appear that more is better when it comes to deciding on the size of your board of directors. Each additional board member brings new contacts and perspective to the table. A bigger Rolodex and more ideas – why not?

Well, it turns out there is a cost to scaling your board. More is not always better. There are two problems that become more significant as boards get larger.

First, scheduling can become a real problem. Institutional investors are often juggling portfolio companies, new investments and relationships with limited partners, making it a challenge to schedule future board meetings.

This can create more than an administrative problem. With too large of a board, you may find that you can't get everyone in the room at the same time, leaving at least one person to lose the benefit of having continuity between meetings. The CEO will always be working to catch somebody up on what was discussed last time.

The second issue with large boards is that they are usually less effective in providing guidance. Have you ever tried to have a discussion in a group of 20 people? It generally doesn't work. You're more likely to have a productive debate about key company issues with a relatively small group. Constructive dialogue dies out once a board reaches a certain size, leaving board meetings to be a one directional update (management updating the board) rather than a highly engaged conversation.

Given these constraints, early-stage companies usually have boards that range in size from five to 10 members. The sweet spot appears to lie at the lower end of the range: five to seven members.

When you're negotiating the structure of your board with an investor, keep these targets in mind.

NOT EVERYONE CAN BE ON THE BOARD – OBSERVER RIGHTS

As aforementioned, large boards can become cumbersome – early-stage firms generally should limit the board to five to seven directors. There are, however, situations where there are more than seven people who feel entitled to having a seat on the board. This might arise when there are numerous founders, angels or VCs involved with the company.

When this happens, you will need to help your constituents negotiate against this constraint. One way to keep some of the involved parties engaged without giving them a board seat is to give them observer rights. Board observers are entitled to attend meetings and participate in the group's leadership, even though they don't have a formal vote on the board.

Board observer rights are also often requested by VCs when boards are not already overcrowded. This right enables them to bring junior members of their team to the meetings to give the junior staff more experience and provide more support for the company.

VC CONTROL PROVISIONS: KEEPING THE RUG UNDER THEM

VCs typically include a series of control provisions as conditions of their investments. Generally, these terms define actions that require approval of preferred shareholders.

These provisions are designed to close loopholes whereby managers can unilaterally mitigate the rights of the investors or put the company in peril. If you're a team player who intends to abide by the spirit of the terms of an investment, these provisions will not present an issue, as ultimately they are provisions that make for a true partnership between investor and operator.

Some common provisions that require approval from the preferred shareholders include:

- Changing the rights of the preferred share class,
- Issuing or buying back shares,
- Issuing a dividend,
- Amending the company's articles of incorporation or by-laws,
- Agreeing to a merger or acquisition of the company, or
- Changing the size or structure of the board of directors.

WHY VCS INVEST IN C-CORPS

When VCs invest in a startup they require the company to be legally formed as c-corps for a variety of reasons. While I am not a lawyer and this is not an exhaustive list, I have attempted to articulate the key reasons for this requirement.

Liability

C-corps appear to provide the strongest corporate veil, minimizing the extent to which investors in the corporation are exposed to the company's liabilities.

Pass Through

Most of the other legal structures do not provide complete separation between the company and its shareholders. Complete separation between the company and shareholders not only provides VCs with greater protection from legal liabilities incurred by the portfolio company, it also simplifies the accounting. Since VC firms are structured as limited partnerships, gains and losses realized by a portfolio company that was not a c-corp (and did not have separation between the company and its shareholders) would be passed through to the limited partners of the VC fund. This additional accounting would create significant work and administrative costs for these limited partners and lead to substantial fluctuations in accounting valuations of the VC portfolio.

Stock Options
C-corps can have stock options plans, which are often valuable tools for recruiting and maintaining talent in a corporation.

Familiarity
C-corps are well-known structures with lots of case law surrounding them, making navigating the legal jungle easier.

Keeping Founders Around

FOUNDER'S EQUITY WILL VEST AFTER VC INVESTMENT

When a VC sends you a term sheet, it will include a clause about the operating founder's equity vesting over time. This means that the founders of the company will not have rights to some or all of their equity stakes until they earn it by working with the company for a period of time.

It's worth noting that in practice this can be implemented as a stock buyback, whereby the company has the right to purchase shares already issued to founders at a pre-determined cost. The percentage of the founder's shares that the company can repurchase declines over time, simulating a traditional vesting schedule.

This seems backward to some new entrepreneurs. How can they lose the rights to something that they already own? There is, however, good reason for the vesting clause.

When an investor backs a company, he is betting on the management team as much (if not more) than the idea or technology. Ideas and technologies don't become companies on their own – entrepreneurs make that happen. Imagine a scenario in which, shortly after a VC invests several million dollars, the management team quits knowing that they have an equity stake in the company. The investors would be left to pull together a new team and face losing their investment.

The objective of this clause isn't to cheat the founders out of their equity. Remember, the good VCs want key operators to have sufficient equity. Rather, the clause is designed to ensure that the founding team has an incentive to stick around and build the company – putting forth the effort that was promised to the investor.

WHAT IS EQUITY VESTING ACCELERATION

While vesting provides key people with an incentive to stay with the company over time, it can leave some concerned that they won't get their fair share if the company is sold quickly. For example, if a founder owns 20 percent of the company and his stake is set to vest over four years (5 percent per year), he might wonder how much he will be paid if the company is sold after the first year. Will he be paid out as if he owns 5 percent or 20 percent (the total amount of equity allocated to him, not all of which had vested)?

The saving grace for individuals exposed to a vesting program is acceleration. An acceleration clause accelerates vesting of stock in pre-defined situations. One commonly pre-defined situation is a change of control, a legal way of describing an acquisition.

If the founder in the scenario above had an acceleration clause that was triggered by this acquisition, he would likely be compensated for owning more than the 5 percent of his shares that had already vested at the time of sale.

EQUITY VESTING ACCELERATION TRIGGERS

While the events that trigger the acceleration of vesting can vary by contract, there are a few common structures.

The first is called single trigger acceleration. In single trigger acceleration, the vesting is accelerated when a change of control (acquisition) occurs. Investors, however, might find giving key managers single trigger acceleration disconcerting. What happens if the acquirer requires the key personnel to stick around through the post-acquisition transition? If these key managers get their payouts on the day the transaction occurs, they may not have an incentive to help out after the acquisition, a risk that can scare of likely acquirers.

As a result, managers who are likely to be key to the transition of the company after its acquisition are typically offered double trigger acceleration. This structure requires two events to take place in order for acceleration to be triggered. First, a change of control must take place. Second, the manager must either work for the acquirer for a pre-determined period or be dismissed by the acquirer. These managers still get their payout, but have an incentive to support the acquirer after the acquisition.

Double trigger acceleration is an important requirement as it can prevent the expectation of selfish behavior from derailing acquisitions.

COMPENSATION THRESHOLDS

When you raise venture capital, your company will typically begin paying you and your team a salary. It is important for you and your team to be compensated so that your collective focus can be on building your business, not looking for part-time jobs to cover your rent.

While fair market salaries are typically appropriate, investors will want to ensure that newly-invested capital is used wisely. Toward this end, most VCs require that the preferred investors on the board approve salaries in excess of a specified threshold. To clarify, individuals can be paid more than this amount, but the preferred investors must approve each compensation package. By providing the cap, management is empowered to make necessary lower-level hires without having to wait for approval, while enabling the board to ensure that no team member is over-compensated.

As a matter of process, these terms shouldn't be too concerning to management so long as the cap is set sufficiently high so as to allow the team to engage in making low- and mid-level hires without seeking approval.

Other Considerations

RIGHT OF FIRST REFUSAL: CONTROLLING SHARES

A right of first refusal (ROFR) gives a shareholder the right to buy shares that another shareholder wants to sell before the shares can be offered to a third party.

The ROFR is very important. The party with the ROFR can acquire more shares in a secondary sale should it wish to do so. Moreover, it is a way to prevent shareholders from selling their positions to third parties whom other shareholders might not welcome. These unwelcome third parties might include financial investors with plans for the company that are at odds with those of the rest of the shareholder base, strategic investors looking for inside information about the company or even competitors.

REGISTRATION RIGHTS: PARTICIPATING IN AN IPO

Registration rights give investors the right to force your company to file for and participate in an initial public offering. While these rights are rather nuanced (and your lawyer can help you understand the details), at a high level, there are only a couple of key concepts you need to understand when raising capital.

Demand rights enable a successful vote of the preferred shareholders to demand that the company file to offer up to a designated percentage of the company's share in a public offering. Typically demand rights do not go into effect until after a specified date – often a few years from the date of the initial investment.

Piggyback registration rights enable investors to participate in the public offering of the company's shares, providing them with an opportunity to obtain liquidity.

It's worth noting that these rights are not frequently invoked in a hostile manner as the investors want the company to pursue an IPO when it is poised to succeed in the public market. As a result, the key purpose of these rights is to ensure that the preferred investors may participate in a public offering at the appropriate time.

After the Deal

THE VC: YOUR NEW PARTNER

I wanted to conclude this guide by reminding you that after the laborious process of raising money the VC switches from being your counterparty in the negotiation to your business partner. As your business partner the VC should make introductions, help you dissect strategic issues, lay a path for growth and generally be a resource to you in this endeavor.

It is very important to remember that this is the relationship that you are trying to develop through the fundraising process. While it is important to negotiate toward a deal that makes you comfortable, be sure to do so in a manner that strengthens your relationship
with the VC.

Conclusion

THE FUNDRAISING PROCESS FOR STARTUPS HAS BEEN TOO
opaque for far too long. My hope is that this book illuminated most of what should happen from the time you decide to raise money until the day you have a full bank account.

By giving entrepreneurs this playbook, I intend to make the fundraising process easier for both entrepreneurs and investors. If entrepreneurs know what to expect, they will be prepared, saving investors time. Furthermore, preparing more effectively ensures that entrepreneurs are judged solely on the merits of their venture, not their ability to guess how the fundraising process works.

If you found this book helpful, you should consider reading my second book on fundraising, *Breaking The Rules*, which is already under construction as I am writing this conclusion. *Breaking The Rules* delves into how to negotiate your financing with investors. Additionally, you can follow my thoughts on Twitter at @mpd or on my blog at http://mpd.me.

Entrepreneurship is the key to mankind's progress. It is the act of transforming invention to innovation. It is what empowers humans to live longer, better and smarter. There are few higher callings. If you are an entrepreneur, continue your march, even in the face of criticism or ridicule. While we won't always succeed, when we do, we make a difference.

Recommended Blogs

CONTINUATIONS By Albert Wenger

ALEX'S TECH THOUGHTS By Alex Taub

AH-HA 2.0 By Ben Sun

INSTIGATOR BLOG By Ben Yoskowitz

BENJI MARKOFF By Benji Markoff

BIJAN SABET By Bijan Sabet

ABOVE THE CROWD By Bill Gurley

FELD THOUGHTS By Brad Feld

CAN I BUY A VOWEL? By Brad Svrluga

THIS IS GOING TO BE BIG By Charlie O'Donnell

CHRIS CALI By Chris Cali

CHRIS DIXON'S BLOG By Chris Dixon

TERM SHEET By Dan Primack

500 HATS By Dave McClure

DAVID B. LERNER By David B. Lerner

WHO HAS TIME FOR THIS? By David Cowan

VENTURE BLOG By David Hornik

FOR ENTREPRENEURS By David Skok

BEYOND VC By Ed Sim

STARTUP LESSONS LEARNED By Eric Ries

FRANCISCO AMADEO By Francisco Amadeo

FRED DESTIN By Fred Destin

AVC By Fred Wilson

GREG ISENBERG By Greg Isenberg

THE JASON CALACANIS WEBLOG By Jason Calacanis

SEEING BOTH SIDES By Jeff Bussgang

BUZZMACHINE By Jeff Jarvis

REDEYE VC By Josh Kopelman

IN OVER YOUR HEAD By Julien Smith

MPD By Mark Peter Davis

BOTH SIDES OF THE TABLE By Mark Suster

VENTURE HACKS By Naval Ravikant &
    Babak Nivi

THE EQUITY KICKER By Nic Brisbourne

GIGAOM By Om Malik

PAUL GRAHAM'S BLOG By Paul Graham

BABBLING VC By Paul Jozefak

INFECTIOUS GREED By Paul Kedrosky

SETH'S BLOG By Seth Godin

VC ADVENTURE By Seth Levine

STEVE'S BLOG By Steve Blank

O'REILLY RADAR By Tim O'Reily

TREVOR OWENS By Trevor Owens

VINICIUS VACANTI By Vinicius Vacanti

PATTERN RECOGNITION By Ian Sigalow

THE GONG SHOW By Andrew Parker

ROB GO By Rob Go

If you want exclusive access to more tips on
startup fundraising and operations sign up
for my email list on http://mpd.me.

Index

3 KEY FUNDRAISING DOCUMENTS

EXECUTIVE SUMMARY (1 PAGE)

- [ ] Name & contact
- [ ] Geographic location
- [ ] Mission statement
- [ ] Pain point
- [ ] Solution
- [ ] Revenue model
- [ ] Market
- [ ] Competitive landscape
- [ ] Milestones
- [ ] Financials/funding
- [ ] Team

PPT PRESENTATION (10–20 SLIDES)

- [ ] Title (1)
- [ ] Team (1)
- [ ] Investment overview (1)
- [ ] Pain point (1-3)
- [ ] Solution (1-5)
- [ ] Revenue model (1-2)
- [ ] Market (1)
- [ ] Competition (1-3)
- [ ] Milestones (1-2)
- [ ] Contact (1)

OPERATIONAL FINANCIAL MODEL

- [ ] Show projections
- [ ] Outputs & inputs
- [ ] Variable-based

FUNDRAISING STEPS

1 1ST CONTACT

» Get the VC's attention: use the right subject
» Do not spam the whole partnership
» Avoid demanding the last minute meeting

2 1ST MEETING

» Bring 2/3 people to explain the "what" and "how"
» Sit on one side of the table
» Explain your business does while highlighting why they'll want to invest
» Explain how you'll make your mission statement come true
» Tell the bigger story
» Solid team introductions explain why a company was started
» Competition: provide insight
» Give and expect straight talk
» Present flexibly
» Ask the VC about follow-on investing

3 AFTER 1ST MEETING

» Respond to VC requests relatively quickly
» Find a 'champion'
» Create momentum
» Maintain momentum: create urgency
» If you can't create interest, move on
» Get your executive summary distributed to other VCs

4 DUE DILIGENCE

» Don't save surprises for after investors commit
» Exploratory meetings: open your kimono
» Customer reference calls
» Filling information gaps: experts
» Sanity check: is your address-able market size realistic?
» Manage VC expectations about operating performance
» Do due diligence on the VC

5 DOING THE DEAL

» The all-partner meeting
» Share your cap table
» Term sheets: exploding offers
» The no shop clause
» Board structure: seeking balance
» Independent director: the tie breaker
» Securing an independent: identify candidates

6 AFTER THE DEAL

» The VC: Your new partner

Made in the USA
Middletown, DE
08 March 2016